C000140735

Roman
Britain

T.W. Potter

Harvard University Press
Cambridge, Massachusetts
1997

© 1983, 1997 The Trustees of
the British Museum

First published 1983
Second edition 1997

Library of Congress Catalog Card
Number: 96-79382

ISBN 0-674-77767-0

Designed by Martin Richards
Cover and series design:
Carroll Associates

Typeset in Van Dijck

Manufactured in China by Imago

Cover illustration: *The Great Dish
from the fourth-century Mildenhall
Treasure. The main frieze is of Bacchus
and his dancing companions. Diameter
60.5 cm (23.8 in).*

Right: *Central roundel of a mosaic
pavement from Leadenhall Street, London,
depicting Bacchus riding a tiger. First-
second century* AD. *Diameter 1.12 m
(43.5 in).*

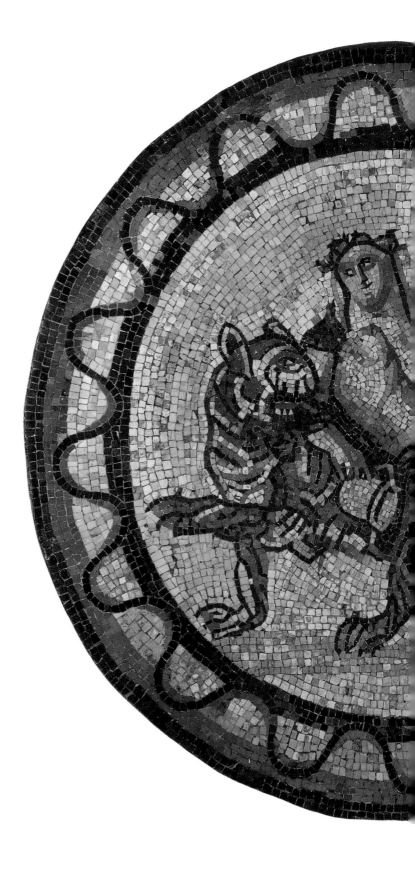

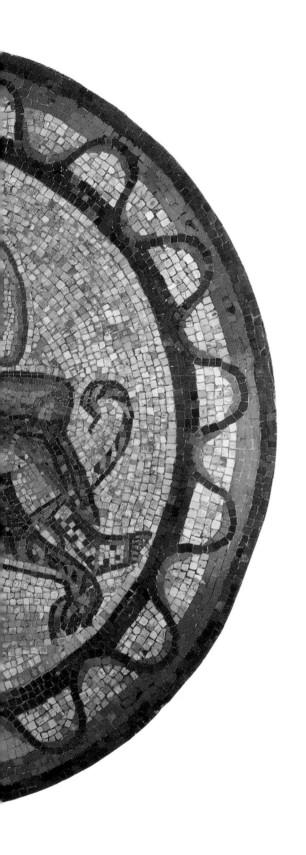

Contents

Acknowledgements

The author and publishers are grateful to the following for permission to reproduce photographs: Cambridge University Collection of Air Photographs p.28 (crown copyright), p. 39 (fig. 19) (crown copyright), p. 40 (crown copyright), p. 51 (crown copyright), p. 87 (copyright reserved); Colchester Archaeological Trust p. 6; English Heritage Photographic Library p. 54 (fig. 37); Hull and East Riding Museum, Hull City Museums, Art Gallery and Archives p.62; Museum of London p. 83.

The photographs on p. 30 and p. 78 (fig. 71) are the copyright of the author. All the other photographs have been provided by the British Museum Photographic Service and are the copyright of the Trustees of the British Museum. The map (p. 4) and the line drawings on pp. 41 and 64 (fig. 49) are by Stephen Crummy.

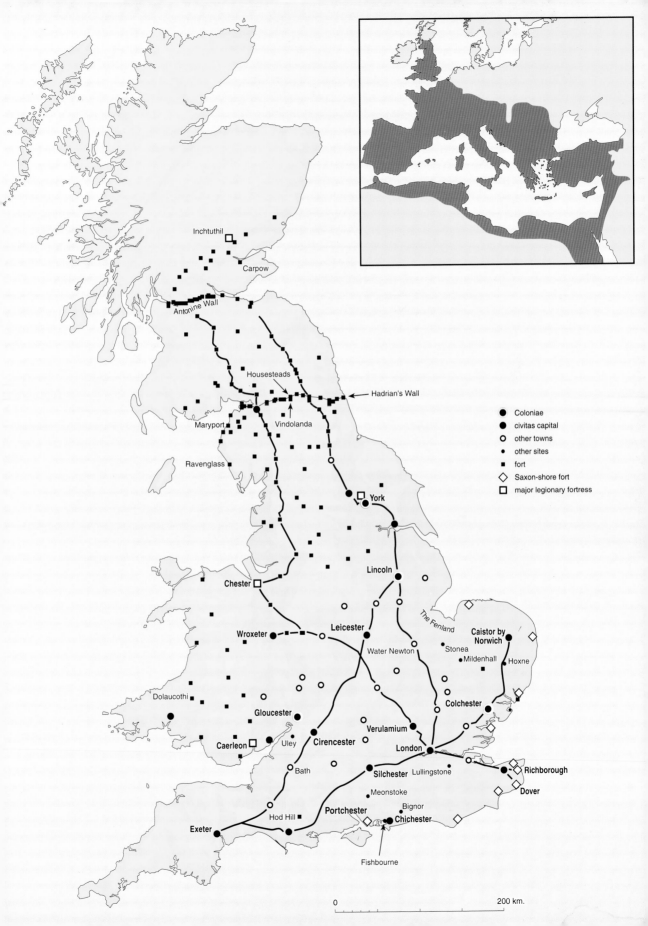

Inchtuthil

Carpow

Antonine Wall

Housesteads

Hadrian's Wall

Maryport

Vindolanda

Ravenglass

Coloniae
civitas capital
other towns
other sites
fort
Saxon-shore fort
major legionary fortress

York

Lincoln

Chester

The Fenland

Caistor by Norwich

Wroxeter

Leicester

Water Newton

Stonea

Mildenhall

Hoxne

Dolaucothi

Gloucester

Colchester

Caerleon

Uley

Cirencester

Verulamium

London

Bath

Silchester

Lullingstone

Richborough

Dover

Meonstoke

Bignor

Hod Hill

Portchester

Chichester

Exeter

Fishbourne

0   200 km.

Introduction

It is the aim of this book to provide the general reader with a brief account of the Roman period in Britain. Although it is not intended to imitate the form of the excellent *Guide to the antiquities of Roman Britain* (British Museum 1958, 1964), the book is illustrated mainly by objects in the very rich British Museum collections, now on show in a completely remodelled display. A number of these are wonderful new discoveries, such as the Thetford Treasure and the Vindolanda writing tablets, made since the Guide was published; but we have also tried to include as many of the famous items in the national collections as possible – and some less well known objects. It is a work that the visitor can carry away as a visual reminder of what he or she has seen, and one which will provide some further background.

It is worth emphasising here that this book is written very much from a Mediterranean viewpoint. This is to underline the fact that Britain was a distant province of a vast empire whose shape and fortune

A fine pavement known as the 'Mosaic of the Wrestling Cupids' (the theme of the central panel), excavated at Middleborough, Colchester in 1979. Measuring 5.8 c. 6.7 m (19 x 22 ft), it dates to c. AD 150-175.

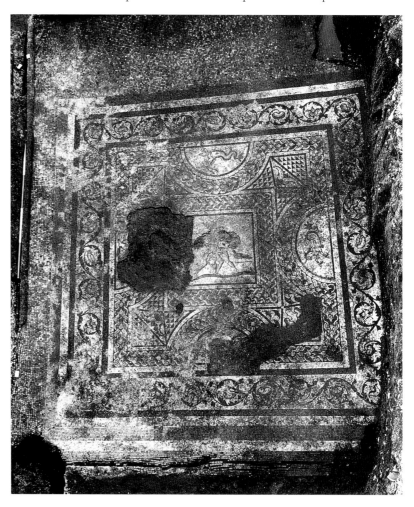

depended ultimately on what happened in Rome itself. All provinces played their part in the history of the empire but they were the rim and spokes of a huge wheel whose hub lay in the centre of Italy. Thus we must attempt to look at Britain mainly (although not exclusively) through Roman eyes; and, at the same time, draw widely upon the often much fuller evidence from other provinces to set matters in perspective.

It remains to pay a very warm general tribute to my colleagues for their help and advice; to Dr Peter Salway, of the Open University, who read some of the chapters in draft; to Christine Barfoot for typing the manuscript; and, above all, to Catherine Johns and Ralph Jackson, who have done an enormous amount towards the preparation of both the text and the illustrations: this is as much their book as it is mine.

1983

This book has been revised to accompany the opening of a completely new Roman Britain room, sponsored by The Weston Foundation, which replaces the gallery of 1983, for which the first edition was written. This has provided the opportunity to incorporate momentous recent discoveries, like the extraordinary Hoxne Treasure, and the equally remarkable Meonstoke building façade, lifted by the Museum in 1989 and now on display for the first time. In addition, while the main structure of the book has been retained, there has been the opportunity to modify and recast views which no longer carry the conviction of fifteen years ago. This shows how the study of Roman Britain remains a vibrant and fascinating subject, as more than thirty million visitors to the gallery that opened in 1983 would seem to confirm. It has been particularly pleasing to learn that many schools have found the first edition of this book to be useful, not least in the context of the British National Curricula. I trust that student and layperson alike will continue to feel that the images and words here presented continue to be a source of interest and stimulation.

To my acknowledgements in the first edition, I would like to add the names of Simon James, for his close scrutiny of the text; to Kate Down, for its preparation; and to Coralie Hepburn for her most helpful editorial work.

1997

Chapter 1 | Britain under the Romans

When the Roman invasion force of some 40,000 men set sail from Gesoriacum, modern Boulogne, in AD 43, they were about to acquire one of Rome's last provinces. It was also to prove one of the more costly and difficult to conquer and control, something that must have been far from the mind of the emperor Claudius when he ordered his army to Britain. Much more pertinent was the fact that a successful war would bring credit and glory to a man unexpectedly elevated to the throne, and with a reputation for little more than physical deformity and obscure scholarship. Moreover, British wealth in minerals, livestock, foodstuffs and slaves might well be ample recompense for the expense (which mattered because Claudius had inherited a near-empty Treasury). This assessment was based on a good deal of intelligence about Britain. Mediterranean traders had been visiting the country from at least as early as the fourth century BC and Caesar had provided a lengthy account of what he saw when he invaded in 55 and 54 BC. After Caesar's day, several plans were drawn up to annexe Britain and in AD 40 an army was actually assembled; but, in the end, it fell to Claudius and his expedition commander, Aulus Plautius, to set events in motion.

At the time of the conquest, Britain was divided up into a number of tribal groups. Broadly speaking, these tribes belonged to a very widespread European group, known to the ancients as the Celts; but we should recognise that, however useful the term 'Celtic' may be, it nevertheless masked a great diversity of peoples. Caesar tells us, for example, that the coastal areas of south-east Britain were populated by Belgae, who had come from Belgium and north-eastern France to plunder and then to settle. Although it is not easy to reconcile the Belgae with the archaeological evidence, these remarks underline the fact that there was a good deal of cross-Channel trade and migration over many centuries before the Roman conquest. Caesar's former ally, Commius, who was chieftain of the Gaulish tribe of the Atrebates (centred around the north French town of Arras), provides a good instance when he fled to Britain in about 50 BC, after unwisely backing the Gallic leader, Vercingetorix, against Caesar. He was to settle at Silchester, ancient Calleva Atrebatum, near Reading, where he was the first ruler in Britain to strike coins inscribed with his name.

Coinage in gold, silver or bronze came into use in parts of south-eastern Britain about 100 BC and became widespread amongst many of the southern tribes in the later part of the first century BC. It is particularly helpful that, following Commius' example, many rulers began to inscribe their coins, so that we can sometimes reconstruct tribal dynasties. Caesar's principal opponent, Cassivellaunus, remains numismatically anonymous; but it is likely that his territory included a large area north of the Thames, with a tribal centre in the vicinity of St Albans, Roman Verulamium. Indeed, Tasciovanus, who became king of the Catuvellauni about 20 BC, issued coins inscribed VER[ulamium].

1 *Bronze coins of two British rulers of the Catuvellauni tribe: Tasciovanus (c. 20 BC-AD 5) and Cunobelinus (c. AD 10-40). Inscribed coins help to reconstruct some of the pre-Roman tribal dynasties.*

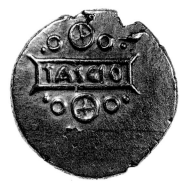

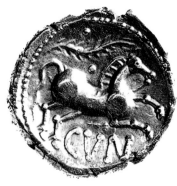

However, it was Tasciovanus' son, Cunobelinus (Shakespeare's Cymbeline), who was to become the best-known and most powerful of the tribal leaders. Taking office about AD 10, he soon afterwards ousted the Trinovantes from their capital at Camulodunum, near modern Colchester, and took over this strongly defended position for himself. The distribution of his coins suggests an extensive kingdom covering Essex and Hertfordshire, but with contacts much further afield. Moreover, it is clear from a wealth of imported objects and commodities, including wine, that he maintained close links with the Roman world. He is very likely to have been one of the native rulers who, according to the Greek writer Strabo, sent embassies to the emperor Augustus in Rome and 'not only dedicated offerings on the Capitol, but have also managed to make the whole of the island virtually Roman property'.

It was certainly in Rome's interests to maintain a stable political situation in Britain. To command the loyalty and friendship of a powerful king such as Cunobelinus must have been seen as an effective way of keeping indirect control. Not that all tribes were under the Catuvellaunian yoke. To mention just a few, the Iceni of Norfolk were apparently a rich and independent group; the Atrebates had a strong and particularly pro-Roman dynasty; the Durotriges of Dorset and Wiltshire clearly lived turbulent lives, to judge from the number of strongly defended hill-top forts in their territory; while, in the north of England, there were the populous Brigantes, most of whom had few dealings with their southern compatriots.

This then was the world that Rome was to bring into the orbit of empire: a divided land of small tribal kingdoms, with a fluctuating balance of power, and a style of life firmly rooted in prehistory. When Cunobelinus died, in AD 40 or 41, it was clearly a good moment to step in before his sons, Caratacus and Togodumnus (who were implacably anti-Roman), could upset the balance. Not that things were to go wholly Rome's way by any means.

The first stages of conquest were comparatively straightforward. The four legions, the IInd Augusta, IXth Hispana, XIVth Gemina and XXth Valeria, together with auxiliary troops, made a successful landing, very likely at Richborough in east Kent, and possibly at Chichester. Resistance there was, but it was soon overcome. Before long the Roman army was in Camulodunum, led by Claudius himself, who was accompanied by some elephants he had brought with him to cow the natives. In Rome, a commemorative arch was built in honour of the

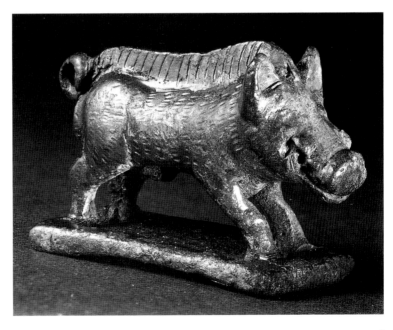

2 Bronze figurine of a boar from Camerton, Somerset. It was found with large quantities of military metalwork of the first century AD, probably from a fort, and could come from a standard of the XXth legion, whose symbol was a boar (see illustration 40). Length 5.6 cm (2.2 in).

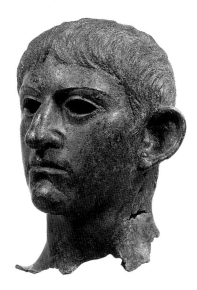

3 *Bronze head of the emperor Claudius (AD 41-54) from the River Alde at Rendham in Suffolk. It has been wrenched off a life-size statue, and probably derived from the nearby colony of army veterans at Camulodunum (Colchester). Height 30 cm (12 in).*

4 *A hoard of silver drinking cups from Hockwold, Norfolk. Silver cups were appropriate for drinking wine, a continental luxury which was already imported into Britain before the Roman conquest. The Hockwold cups had been deliberately crushed before burial, and are seen here in their restored condition. First century AD.*

emperor, and it proclaimed that Claudius 'subdued eleven kings of Britain without any reverse, and received their surrender, and was the first to bring barbarian nations beyond the ocean under Roman sway'. All in all, it was a great triumph, which Claudius exploited as fully as possible.

In Britain the flanks were rapidly secured by establishing 'client kingdoms'– namely ones ruled by friendly kings – in the territories of the Iceni of Norfolk and the Regni of southern Sussex. Chichester was to develop into the centre of the southern kingdom – and its ruler, Tiberius Claudius Cogidumnus, was made a Roman citizen, as his three names show. Then, a three-pronged line of attack was launched: one towards Lincoln, another north-west towards Leicester and a third to the south-west. Here, amongst twenty native towns (*oppida*) that were taken, was the great hill-fort of Maiden Castle near Dorchester, where excavation has revealed a war-cemetery of corpses, perhaps of this time, some gruesomely slain. By AD 47, the advance temporarily settled along

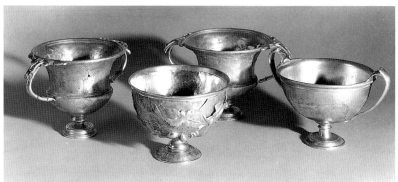

a road, the Fosse Way, which ran from Exeter to Lincoln and the Humber. This was not a frontier as Hadrian's Wall was to be, for no Roman of this time would have believed in the concept of finite boundaries; but it did mark a suitable breathing-space, coinciding too with a change in commander from Aulus Plautius to Ostorius Scapula. Meanwhile, a network of military bases was laid down, spreading a garrison of legionary detachments and auxiliary troops across the conquered area and leaving the XXth legion to secure the rear from a fortress at Camulodunum, today buried beneath the streets and houses of modern Colchester.

What respite there was did not last long. It was known that native resistance would be strong, particularly from the tribes of Wales; but a move forward was necessary, if only to bring under Roman control the rich mineral deposits of western Britain. As a first step, the peoples within what was already Roman territory were disarmed, provoking a short-lived and easily suppressed revolt by the Iceni. The XXth legion was moved out of Colchester (where a town for retired legionaries was created, a *colonia*) to a forward base, probably near Gloucester, and an attack was mounted against the Deceangli of north Wales. It was to be the first of a series of long, difficult campaigns, lasting for a decade or more, and involving four governors. Ostorius Scapula probably had the

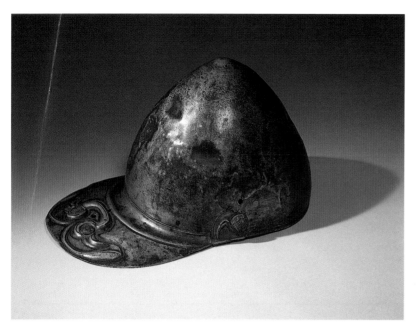

5 *The so-called Meyrick helmet, probably found in the north of England. Datable to the second half of the first century AD, it is of Roman shape with Celtic-style decoration, and was presumably owned by an auxiliary soldier. Height 16.7 cm (6.6 in).*

hardest task but he achieved a great success when Caratacus, Cunobelinus' surviving son and the principal leader of British resistance, was handed over to the Romans by the treacherous Brigantian queen, Cartimandua (who was no doubt currying favour as a way of gaining Roman support in her politically divided kingdom). But it is a measure of the Roman army's success to see how forts and roads gradually spread over Wales and south-west England. Much of the opposition had been beaten down, not least the fiercely bellicose Silures; nevertheless a military presence was needed to complete the conquest of Wales and to maintain a firm Roman hold.

Late in AD 58 Suetonius Paulinus became governor. After some initial campaigning in Wales, he decided that the moment was right to launch an attack upon the island of Anglesey. It was in the aftermath of a triumphant victory that Paulinus learned of the outbreak of a rebellion which all but saw the end of Roman Britain. The main protagonist was Queen Boudicca (or Boudica, but erroneously known as Boadicea, due to misreadings of old manuscripts), widow of the king of the Iceni, Prasutagus. Upon her husband's death, in AD 60, she had been humiliated and her daughters raped, while her people had for nearly two decades borne oppressive taxes and insufferable Roman arrogance. Still worse was the fate of their Trinovantian neighbours, numbers of whom had had their land taken over by overbearing Roman veteran soldiers, when the *colonia* of Camulodunum was founded in AD 49. The last straw was the decision of Roman money-lenders to reclaim their loans, made on a large scale in the years following the conquest: the only apparent solution was to rise up against the Roman yoke.

The course of the revolt can be traced both in the pages of the ancient historians, Tacitus and Dio Cassius, and from the evidence of excavation. Thick layers of burning in Colchester, London and

Verulamium (near modern St Albans) mark the sacking of these towns as, almost unopposed, the Iceni and Trinovantes swept first southwards and then northwards to meet Suetonius Paulinus and his comparatively tiny force of 10,000 men. The battle joined, discipline and experience had its way; the Britons were routed, leaving 80,000 for dead. Boudicca committed suicide and the revolt was over.

It is not difficult to imagine the punitive measures that the Romans took following the suppression of the uprising: recent history provides too many parallels. But it is encouraging that for once wise counsel eventually prevailed. A sympathetic finance-officer (procurator), Julius Classicianus, was installed, Paulinus was recalled soon afterwards and a new governor was appointed. So successful was the new policy of rehabilitation that, by AD 67, one of the four legions (the XIVth Gemina) and some auxiliary troops had been withdrawn. However, Rome was beginning increasingly to look towards the north of England, where the once-unified Brigantes were now locked in internal strife. The root of the problem was that Queen Cartimandua had fallen out with her one-time consort, Venutius, so dividing the Brigantes into two main factions.

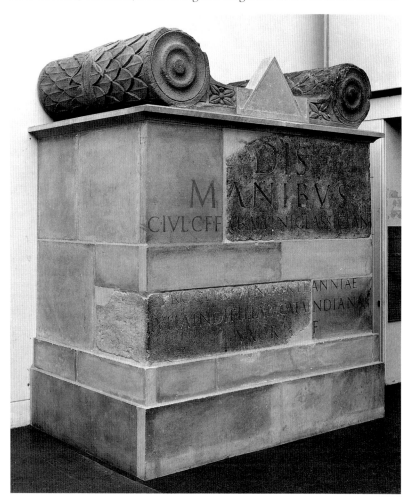

6 *The tombstone of Gaius Julius Alpinus Classicianus, who was sent to Britain as procurator (finance minister) in the aftermath of the rebellion led by Queen Boudicca in AD 60-61. Found at London, this monumental tomb, some 2.28 m (7 ft 6 in) in length, was set up by his wife (uxor). Dis manibus means 'to the spirits of the departed', and was commonly abbreviated to 'D.M.'.*

This was reason enough to intervene, but the aims may well have been more long term. Campaigning began about AD 70 under Vettius Bolanus, and was continued by his successor, Petillius Cerealis (AD 71-4) and probably by Julius Frontinus (AD 74-8). The legionary fortress at York (Eboracum) was founded early in this period, as was a fort at Carlisle, and a measure of control established; but it was not until Britain's most famous Roman governor, Gnaeus Julius Agricola, took over that a truly decisive move was made.

Agricola is particularly well known to us because we possess a detailed biography written by the ancient historian Tacitus. That Tacitus was Agricola's son-in-law has often seemed reason to assume that the book is full of prejudice in Agricola's favour: but, if not a mature work of scholarship, there is nevertheless sufficient circumstantial detail to show that the governor was a man of extraordinary energy and of very considerable abilities. Thirty-eight years of age when he took up the governorship in AD 78, he had already served twice in Britain and knew the country and its problems well. He was in the field almost as soon as he arrived, with a campaign in north Wales and in Anglesey (where, nearly twenty years on from Paulinus' expedition, a new generation of anti-Roman tribesmen had grown up). A legionary fortress was completed at Chester, and he then turned his attention to the north. By the end of AD 79, a two-pronged attack up either side of the Pennines had taken his army to the Tyne-Solway isthmus – the Newcastle to Carlisle line – where Hadrian's Wall was later to be built. A major base was constructed at Red House near Corbridge and there was already one at Carlisle: these were springboards for a sustained campaign into Scotland, which began the following year. Towards the end of AD 80, the army had reached the Forth-Clyde line (from Edinburgh to Glasgow) and, by the same date, Agricola had made considerable progress – as we shall see in subsequent chapters – in bringing about 'Romanisation' in the south of the province.

Aerial photography and excavation serve to confirm Tacitus' account in that they have disclosed an extensive network of forts of this period, spread over much of the conquered territory. However, campaigning was by no means over. Following a programme of consolidating their position and a season's fighting in south-west Scotland, the army then struck further northwards. Along the Scottish lowlands, a series of marching camps, forts and a legionary fortress at Inchtuthil, on the River Tay not far from Perth, mark the progress of the Roman forces. Skilfully using the fleet to reconnoitre ahead and to carry out commando-type raids, Agricola's army eventually reached a still unidentified point in north-east Scotland, Mons Graupius. Here, in AD 84, the final showdown took place. It was a hard-fought battle but, at the end of the day, 10,000 Britons lay dead and only 360 Roman soldiers, and the British had dispersed in ignominious defeat. It was a good moment for Agricola to end his period of service, handing over, as Tacitus remarks, 'a province peaceful and secure to his successor'.

In truth, this was of course hardly the case, since the Scottish Highlands, although monitored by a strong garrison at the mouths of

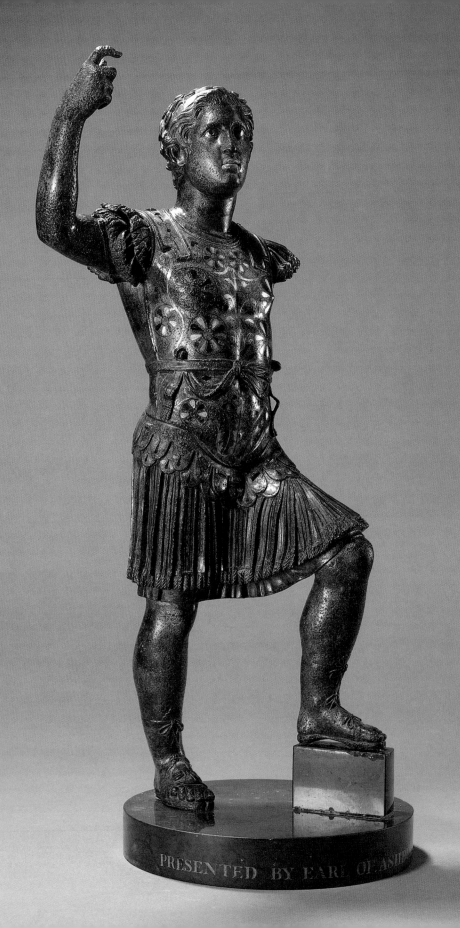

PRESENTED BY EARL OF ASHB[...]

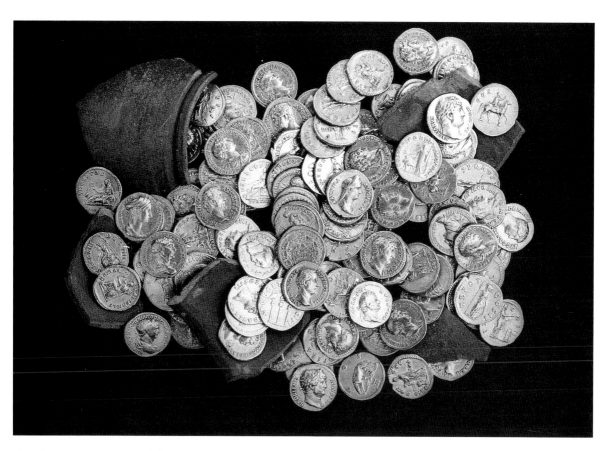

the glens, were never subdued. But archaeology does support Tacitus when elsewhere he sourly observes that 'the conquest of Britain was completed and straightaway let slip'. This much is clear from excavations upon the fortress at Inchtuthil, and at nearby forts, which show that, around AD 87, they were systematically dismantled. The reasons for this cannot be closely identified; but we do know that the Danube provinces were under heavy attack at this time, and that the Roman army was therefore over-stretched. In this context, the conquest of Scotland – a poor area, highly resentful of Rome – must have seemed a low priority. The retreat was gradual but, by about AD 100, the northern boundary of Rome's British province had settled upon a strongly protected road-line, the Stanegate, which ran a little to the south of Hadrian's Wall. Few Romans could have known it, but the decision to consolidate the position at this point represented a crucial change in thinking; the grandiose ideas of the first Roman emperor, Augustus, of an infinite empire, were slowly disappearing, to be replaced by a concept of a world where the 'barbarians' were to be divided from the Romans. This is a story that we shall trace in subsequent chapters.

8 *A hoard of 126 gold coins, found in 1995 and buried in a pot about AD 160 in south Oxfordshire. Ranging in date from issues of Nero (AD 54-68) to Antoninus Pius (AD 138-161), it is only the fourth second-century hoard of gold coins to be discovered in Britain.*

7 Opposite *Bronze statuette of the emperor Nero (AD 54-68) said to be from Barking Hall, Suffolk, but probably from Baylham Mill near Ipswich. Embellished with silver, niello and copper inlay, the emperor is shown in the guise of Alexander. Height 56 cm (22 in).*

Chapter 2 | The people of Roman Britain

There is a common tendency to think of the Roman episode of British history as a period when the population included a great many people from Italy. Nothing could be further from the truth. Whilst the presence of a Roman civil service and of a large army of occupation guaranteed a substantial number of foreigners, even these were made up of people drawn from all over the empire. Moreover, although it is impossible to arrive at any precise figures, it is nevertheless quite certain that the great majority of the population was made up of Britons, some of whom became very Romanised, while others – particularly in the uplands – were affected hardly at all. Even with the arrival of the Germanic peoples in the fifth century, it is now believed that there was relatively little major change to the composition of the people of Britain.

That said, our sources cannot be described as full: a meagre supply of written testimony by ancient authors; something over two thousand inscriptions upon stone, many of them fragmentary; and other inscriptions and graffiti, mostly very brief, upon pottery, metalwork, wood, wall-plaster and the like. One has only to wander over many north African or east Mediterranean sites, where countless inscribed altars and dedications still litter the ground, to appreciate how little written mate-

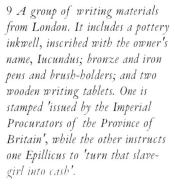

9 A group of writing materials from London. It includes a pottery inkwell, inscribed with the owner's name, Iucundus; bronze and iron pens and brush-holders; and two wooden writing tablets. One is stamped 'issued by the Imperial Procurators of the Province of Britain', while the other instructs one Epillicus to 'turn that slave-girl into cash'.

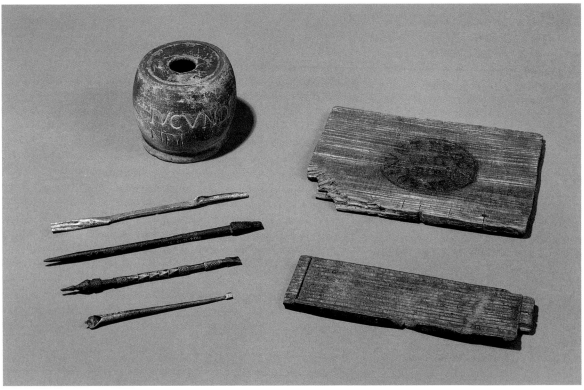

rial concerning Roman Britain has come down to us. Nevertheless, there is much that can be said, aided not least by the remarkable discovery of letters and archival records, conserved on sheets and tablets of wood, found at the fort of Vindolanda, near Hadrian's Wall. With now some 250 substantial texts, these do contain much unique information.

Two features of our sources are particularly helpful. One is the fact that tombstones often give details of the deceased's age and origin (and,

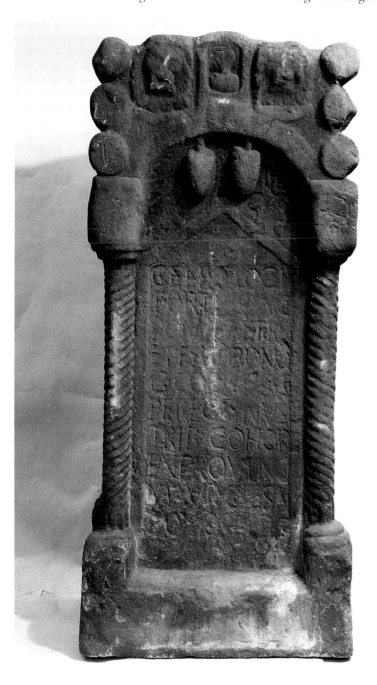

10 *An altar from the fort at Maryport, Cumbria. It is poignantly dedicated to Fortune the Home-bringer by Gaius Cornelius Peregrinus, tribune, who came from a town called Saldae, modern Bejaia in north-eastern Algeria. Height 1.52 m (60 in).*

in the case of a soldier, of his career). To take a famous example from South Shields, we have a tombstone set up by one Barates, who came from Palmyra in Syria and whose own memorial shows him to have apparently been a dealer in flags and ensigns. He lived to the good age of sixty-eight, but his wife, who was a British girl of the Catuvellaunian tribe, that is from Hertfordshire, died when she was only thirty. She is described as a freedwoman, and it is quite reasonable to suppose that it was her future husband who had liberated her from slavery. Inscriptions such as this can therefore be highly informative documents. Others may also be moving, such as an altar dedicated at the fort of Maryport (Cumbria) by C. Cornelius Peregrinus. He was a staff officer who was clearly feeling homesick for his native Saldae (Bejaia in Algeria) when he had inscribed 'to Fortune the Homebringer' as part of the dedication. Similarly, a Vindolanda letter requests that 'you send the things that I need for the use of my boys ... which you well know I cannot properly get hold of here'.

The names alone can also be very useful sources of evidence. From about the time of the conquest of Britain, it became customary for full Roman citizens to possess three names. The first was the *praenomen* or given name (e.g. Marcus); the second was the *nomen gentilicium* or family surname; while the third was the *cognomen*, which, in origin, was a private nickname. However, as more and more people were granted citizenship, so it became commonplace to take the family name of the emperor as the *nomen*. Thus, when the client king of the Chichester area, Cogidumnus,

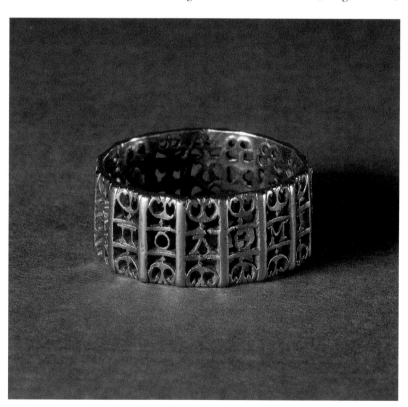

11 *A gold ring from the military base at Corbridge, Northumberland. It bears the words in Greek, 'love-charm of Polemius', a reminder of the cosmopolitan nature of society in many parts of the ancient world.*

was made a Roman citizen, he called himself Tiberius Claudius Cogidumnus, in honour of the emperor Claudius for granting him the franchise. This is not just a useful index of who was and who was not a Roman citizen, however; it is also an indication of when a family acquired citizen status, and, as long as the name was not completely changed, a clue to the origin of that family. Cogidumnus is very clearly a Briton, while others just as clearly came from Italy, Africa, and elsewhere. Indeed often – as with Barates and his wife – a place of origin is specifically mentioned, there being some 135 examples known from Britain alone. Nearly every part of the empire is referred to, but Germany and then Italy are the provinces most commonly cited.

Most people were of insufficient status to aspire to be Roman citizens. Thus, we should remember that, casual graffiti apart, those affluent enough to pay for tombstones and dedications belonged to the upper echelons of society, so that our picture is at best a very biased one. The point may be well brought out by a brief glance at some of the different classes of people described for us in our sources. Leaving aside emperors, both the governors and the commanders of the legions came from the top rank of Roman society, namely senatorial families (although this picture does alter in the later centuries of the Roman empire). Between AD 43 and AD 213, about which time Britain was divided into two provinces, some thirty-eight governors are known, out of a likely total of more than fifty. What we know of their careers shows them to have been highly experienced, talented men. For example, Agricola, who was governor between AD 78 and 84 and is the best documented case, had already served twice in Britain, once as a legionary officer and later as commander of the XXth legion. He had also governed Aquitania in south-west Gaul, and was consul in Rome immediately prior to his British appointment. Experience in both military command and in government was regarded as an essential background, particularly with so large an army of occupation to manage. Most of the early governors were Italian by origin – Agricola, who came from Fréjus (Forum Iulii) in southern Gaul, is an exception – but, in the early second century, this began to change. From the emperor Trajan onwards (who, like his successor Hadrian, came from Spain), the principate was largely filled by people of provincial origin, a feature that applied to other high-ranking posts. Thus, Lollius Urbicus, who came from Tiddis in Numidia and led campaigns into Scotland in the early AD 140s, was one of several north African governors of Britain around this time. It is a sign of the way that Italy began to lose its pre-eminence, in favour of a more integrated empire where social advancement was possible whatever one's country of birth.

Much the same pattern can be discerned from the army appointments. Here, from a predominance of Italians in the first century AD, we see a much more cosmopolitan selection of officers taking up the senior posts in the course of the second century. The way in which the army was structured, with its heavy reliance upon 'auxiliary' units made up of non-citizens, recruited from all over the empire and even beyond, will be examined in a subsequent chapter. Here we may note the extraordinary geographical diversity in the origins of both officers and men in this

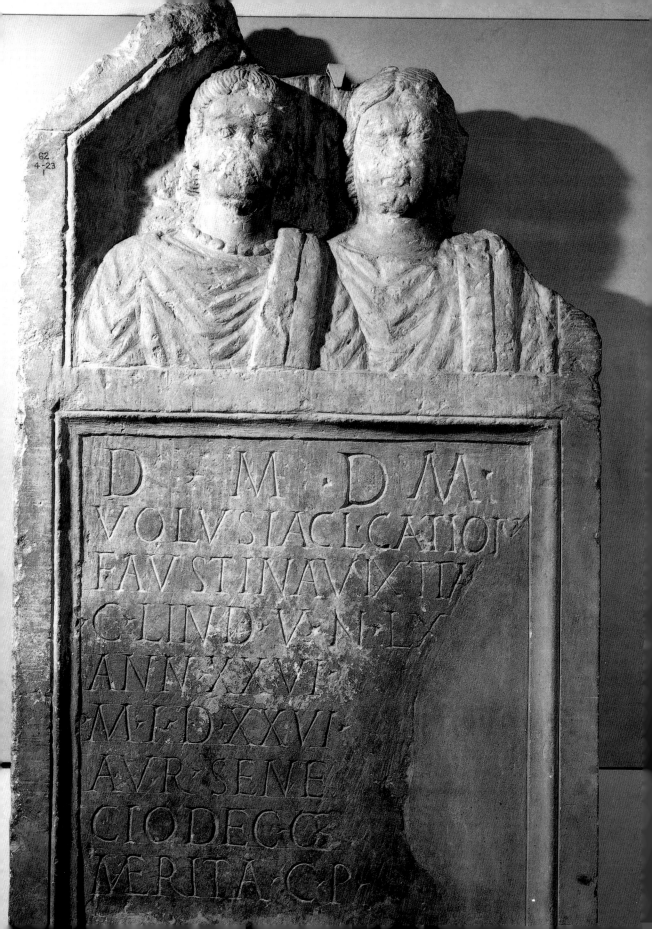

D · M · D · M ·
VOLVSIA C LCATIO
FAVSTINA VIXIT
C IIND V N LX
ANN XXVI
M · I · D XXVI
AVR · SENE
CIO DE C C
MERITA C P

middle period of the province's history, followed by an increasing tendency for the communities that grew up outside the forts to provide the manpower of the late-Roman garrisons.

In addition to the army, there was a substantial body of civil servants. Apart from the governor, the most important officer was the procurator. He was responsible directly to the emperor, whose estates, mines and other property he supervised, and he dealt with the *annona*, the levy of grain that supplied the army, and the army's pay. But his principal duty was to manage the overall finances of the province, namely to receive taxes on land and individuals. For this reason, a periodic census was necessary and special officers were sometimes appointed to carry it out; an example is a commander of the regiment, the Second Cohort of Asturians, Cn. Munatius Aurelius Bassus, who was seconded to sort out the facts and figures of the Roman citizens of Camulodunum. Much depended, however, on the character of the procurator and his staff. As the historian Tacitus implies, they were not above graft and dishonesty, just as it was the rapacious measures of the procurator, Decianus Catus, which helped to spark off the Iceni rebellion led by Queen Boudicca. By contrast, his successor, Julius Classicianus, was seen as a fair and just man, though he won no praise from Tacitus for sending an adverse report to the emperor Nero about the repressive activities of the governor, Suetonius Paulinus – a report which ultimately resulted in Paulinus' recall. Classicianus was by origin a provincial from Gaul and his wife was the daughter of a noble of the Trier region of Germany; he may therefore have had some sympathy for the plight of the Britons. Like many procurators, he was an *eques*, 'knight', an order of society that ranked a little below the senatorial group, although the sons of *equites* frequently entered the senate.

To the elite groups of the senators and the *equites*, we should add a third important class of people, the decurions or 'curial' class. We shall examine their role in more detail in a chapter on towns, but we may note here that they were councillors, who met in the *curia* or town council chamber. There were several criteria for qualification, amongst them age (twenty-five to fifty-five years) and the size of their fortune. They had of necessity to be men of wealth since their rank meant that they were expected to contribute to the costs of developing a town from their own pockets. Onerous though this obligation must have been, there were advantages to being a decurion; a political career might follow and there was also the question of prestige. Hence the proud tombstone of Volusia Faustina, 'a citizen of Lindum [Lincoln] who lived 26 years, one month and 26 days', set up by her husband, Aurelius Senecio, decurion. Sadly, we have the details of all too few of these decurions or of their fellow townsfolk. Some *seviri augustales* – members of organisations that promoted emperor-worship – are known, like M. Aurelius Lunaris, *sevir* of York and Lincoln, while the freedman status of many *seviri* is underlined by an incomplete inscription recently found at Lincoln, reading '...freedman of the emperor rebuilt the temple on account of his appointment to the sevirate'. Nevertheless, graffiti and lead curse tablets give us a wide range of names. They are mainly a mixture of Celtic and Roman, like the

12 *The tombstone of Volusia Faustina (shown on the left), who was the wife of a town councillor (decurion), Aurelius Senecio. Only twenty-six years, one month and twenty-six days old when she died, she is described as* c. Lind., *citizen of Lincoln, where the memorial was found. Height 1.35 m (4 ft 5 in).*

lead tablets from Bath where no fewer than three women, Velvinna, Germanilla and Jovina, and five men, Exsupereus, Severinus, Augustalis, Comitianus and Catusminianus, are cursed for depriving the anonymous writer of his sweetheart, Vilbia. Make them dumb, the writer urges. Other graffiti are more humorous like the example on a tile from London, 'Austalis has been wandering off on his own every day for a fortnight'.

Our inscriptions also tell us of merchants, craftsmen and slaves. Merchants were not generally highly regarded in the ancient world and we should not assume that they were in any sense comparable to the wealthy businessmen of today. But some like Barates of Palmyra or Lunaris (whose altar was found at Bordeaux) must have achieved some affluence and could seek to improve their status by taking up offices like the sevirate. Craftsmen, some of whom formed guilds, are better known since many, such as some potters, stamped their products. As one might expect, Celtic names far outnumber Latin ones, and very few have the three names that distinguish a Roman citizen. Most were very ordinary people, like Candidus who made tiles for Cirencester, and Clementinus who manufactured fluetiles for Silchester.

Slavery is more difficult to quantify; furthermore, it is a subject emotively coloured for all of us by the slave trade of recent centuries. In antiquity, most saw slavery as the natural order of things, and certainly not a matter for concern. Indeed, some slaves could and did achieve positions of influence and responsibility and there was, of course, always the possibility of becoming by one route or another a freedman. We know from the writer Strabo that Britain exported slaves before the conquest and there is direct evidence for their existence in Roman Britain: for instance, a famous letter found at London where one Rufus instructs someone called Epillicus to 'turn that slave-girl into cash'; or a tombstone from Bath, put up by a British freedwoman to her husband, who had presumably given her freedom through marriage. Like many slaves, she had been given a Greek name, Trufosa (Latinised to Trifosa), meaning 'dainty', 'delicious' – a slave-trader's epithet, no doubt, for a very pretty girl-slave, for whom her master fell.

Even so, we have no real idea of how important slavery was in Roman Britain. It may well have been common, in accordance with Roman practice. Indeed, Tacitus tells how the governor Agricola encouraged the speaking of Latin and the wearing of classical costume so that 'the toga was everywhere to be seen'. Sculptural representations of people, and Latin graffiti are just two areas of evidence that support this observation, leaving no doubt that the middle and upperclass Roman Briton was no rustic outsider. One writer, Ausonius, who came from Bordeaux in France, may not have thought much of them, as his supercilious ditty about a British poet called Silvius Bonus, Silvius the Good, shows:

> What? Silvius Good?
> No Briton could
> Be – better he had
> Been Silvius Bad

But whether or not Silvius was *bonus* or *malus*, many Britons will have thought of themselves as Romans. This is not to say that Celtic culture and language were allowed to die away, for there is good reason to think that all educated Britons were bilingual and that many of the peasant farmers of the north and west probably spoke Latin a little or not at all. Latin was the language of government, law, education and Roman culture, while Celtic British was the language of the family and the countryside. Indeed, the fact that an army of occupation maintained a continual presence in many areas for over three centuries suggests a continuing of the degree of resistance to Roman authority. No neat generalisations should be allowed to mask the deep complexity of Romano-British society, a complexity which despite our many sources we can only dimly perceive.

It remains to add a final point. Of necessity, we have looked at Britain under the Romans very much as it was in the first two centuries of provincial rule. We should, however, remember that there were far-reaching legal and administrative changes in the later Roman period, which, as we shall see in later chapters, had major consequences for some classes of the population. Not least was the division of the province into first two and later four and then five separate provinces, combined with alterations in the structure of government; and the Edict of Caracalla, of about AD 212, which by giving citizenship to all free inhabitants, swept away the most basic social division of the Roman world.

Chapter 3 | Towns

'From Chaironeia two-and-a-half miles brings you to the city of Panopeus in Phokis [Greece]: if you can call it a city where it has no state buildings, no training ground, no theatre and no market square, where it has no running water at a water-head and they live on the edge of a torrent in hovels like mountain huts.'

Pausanias' remarks, written about AD 160, have much to tell us about what Mediterranean people in the ancient world thought a town should look like. It was a view shaped over many centuries. As an example we can cite the Greek colony of Megara Hyblaea in eastern Sicily where, as early as the eighth century BC, public buildings were being grouped around a reserved open space (agora) in the centre of the settlement; and where, soon afterwards, a regular grid of streets was laid out. This notion of regular planning was soon being imitated in other Greek 'new towns', with the agora becoming in effect a civic centre for assemblies, entertainment and ceremony and, of course, a market place. During the fifth century BC, Hippodamos of Miletus, who built Piraeus, Athens' harbour town, and who was thought of by later Greeks as the father of town-planning, codified the experience of several centuries of town-building. It was a crucial step, for it was to influence the way that people thought about a town's appearance for many centuries to come.

Hippodamian principles soon became widespread. Rome itself grew up in an unplanned and haphazard manner, as one might expect in a city that emerged out of a settlement first occupied well before 1000 BC. But its neighbours, the Etruscans (from whom the Romans learned so much about water-management and civil engineering), were soon laying out their new towns and even some of their cemeteries on organised lines. Thus it was that when Rome began to expand its territorial holdings through wars of conquest, there was a well-defined urban model to follow. Just as the Greeks and the Phoenicians had, in their day, sent out colonists to found carefully designed and organised cities, so the Roman authorities decided that in many areas a system of colonies best suited the development of their newly acquired lands. This is not to say that existing towns were pulled down (although this did occasionally happen in regions where they were seen as a focus of opposition); or that the native aristocracy was necessarily dispossessed of its property. Rather, the new colonies (coloniae), populated by Roman citizens or by citizens chosen from their Latin allies, were seen as instruments both of Romanisation and as a way of imposing authority. Appian, writing in the second century AD, puts it as follows: 'As the Romans subjugated the people of Italy successively, it was their habit to confiscate a portion of land and establish towns on it, and to enrol colonists of their own in the towns already on it. They intended these for strongholds ... either to hold the earlier inhabitants in subjection or to repel enemy inroads.'

It is no accident therefore that, in the later years of the Roman Republic, particularly the second and first centuries BC, many of their colonies took on a distinctly military flavour. Often designed to imitate the layout of an army camp, most of them were populated by retired army veterans – landless men who, as the wars of conquest spread to overseas, became an increasingly significant part of the population. The emperor Augustus, writing about 2 BC, records founding colonies of soldiers in no fewer than ten provinces, as well as twenty-eight settlements in Italy itself. Many were to become important cities of today, like Aosta, Turin and Florence. These were chartered towns, where the great majority of the inhabitants were Roman citizens with all the rights, privileges (and duties) to which holders of this rank were entitled. They were also seen as official units of government, in effect small city-states controlling their own land around the town, but nevertheless legally subordinate to the city of Rome.

In part this system worked well, since the people in the areas that were first colonised were familiar with the classical concept of a town: the city-state was the accepted norm. In the northern world of the Celtic Gauls and Britons, on the other hand, matters were organised rather differently. Instead of a network of city-states, there was a tribal structure, dominated by an aristocratic warrior class made up of what Julius Caesar calls *equites*, 'knights'. Whilst there were many large settlements (*oppida*), they were a far cry from those of the Mediterranean world. The majority were situated on hill-tops or on promontories, with strong natural defences that were enhanced by artificial fortifications. Few had a regular layout, and no example is known of anything approaching the civic centre of a classical city. Nevertheless, settlements like the tribal capital Camulodunum, near Colchester, did trade with the Roman world

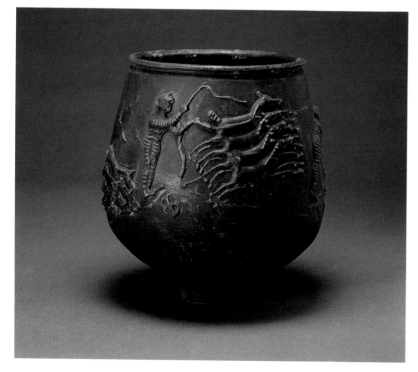

13 *A colour-coated pottery beaker from Colchester, showing four horse-drawn chariots racing around an arena. The charioteers wear long-sleeved jerkins and trousers. Circuses are so far unattested in Britain, but could have existed at important towns like Camulodunum (Colchester). Height 13.5 cm (5.25 in).*

and mint their own coinage, suggesting that their tribal structure was beginning to organise itself into something based on more recognisably urban units.

To Roman eyes, many of these sites must have appeared inconvenient and inaccessible – Camulodunum is in fact a rare exception – so that the existing network of settlements was very largely ignored. Instead, as excavation is currently making clear, they constructed a network of forts and fortresses over the territory they had conquered. In choosing the sites, they had in mind not just the existing political geography (and hence possible foci of opposition), but also the need for good communications; valley locations at easy river crossings were particularly favoured. But what is remarkable about these military foundations is that, as they became redundant with the establishment of peaceful conditions and the push forward by the army towards the west and north, so many of them developed into civilian towns.

It is a process that is not difficult to understand. Although many of the military camps were short-lived, especially in the south-east of Britain, they nevertheless provided a large captive market of men with money in their pockets; on commercial grounds alone there was good reason to set up shop near a fort or fortress. Thus, to take one instance, we can detect a gradual abandonment of the native centre at Bagendon in favour of the vicinity of the fort site 5 km (3 miles) away in the valley of the River Churn at Cirencester. On the other hand, it is inconceivable that, once a military site was evacuated by the army, people were able to take over the fort without official permission; after all, the land must have been regarded as state property. We can therefore suppose that, once the decision to leave a fort had been made, certain sites were designated as civilian centres and the population encouraged to settle there. Indeed, there are hints of this in the half-timbered houses and shops of the earliest period at St Albans (Verulamium), which so closely reflect contemporary military building-styles that architects trained in Roman traditions may have been involved; and at the *coloniae* at Colchester and Gloucester, where the first colonists took over what were, in effect, the converted barracks of the evacuated legionary fortresses.

This brings us on to the different categories of town, something which had important legal implications in the Roman world. The highest rank of town was the *colonia* which, as we have seen, was intended as an important instrument of Romanisation in the empire and was populated by full Roman citizens. The earliest *colonia* in Britain was founded about AD 49 at Colchester; but there were two later foundations, one at Lincoln (about AD 90) and the other at Gloucester (AD 96–8), while York was elevated to the status of a *colonia* sometime before AD 237. Tacitus recounts that Colchester was a 'strong settlement of ex-soldiers ... to protect the country against revolt and to familiarise the provincials with law-abiding government', and, elsewhere, how it became a symbol of 'servitude' to the Britons. Certainly, while both archaeological and historical evidence tells us that the fortifications of the fortress were levelled, the public buildings – particularly a great temple built in classical style and dedicated to the worship of the emperor Claudius – were clearly designed to impress and overawe the native population. As so often, the Romans were using architecture as a form of propaganda.

Other towns were, legally speaking, of lower rank. Only one *municipium* is known for certain, namely Verulamium (St Albans), for it is so described by Tacitus. This was a title given to a Romanised town and its territory, where the inhabitants were self-governing and held rights of citizenship, but normally those of Rome's Latin allies, rather than those of full Roman citizens. However, while *municipia* (and *coloniae*) were very common in many provinces – several hundreds in north Africa, for example – they are generally rare in the northern provinces of Gaul and Britain. This is because, in an area dominated by an existing tribal structure, Romans preferred to impose a system based on what they called the *civitas*. This is not an easy term to define in present-day language, partly because legal definitions of citizenship and non-citizenship changed with the passing of the centuries: but, in effect, it was a status granted to lower-privileged groups of non-Roman citizens, who, nevertheless, exercised a certain degree of autonomy. To the Roman mind, it was the first stage in bringing about urbanisation, although it applied equally to a region as to an individual centre of population. And so it was in Roman Britain, except that many of the towns that came into being were to take on the role as a centre of tribal territory, a form of city-state.

This much is made clear by the names of some of the towns. For instance, the Roman *civitas* at Caistor-by-Norwich was Venta Icenorum – 'the market of the Iceni' – just as modern Paris, in origin a civitas, takes its name from that of the tribe, the Parisii, not from the Celtic designation of the place, Lutetia. Of the towns themselves, there was a characteristically firm attempt to make them as Roman in form as possible. Thus Roman architects seem to have been on hand in the early years after the conquest, and there was certainly official encouragement to adopt Roman ways. This applied particularly to the indigenous aristocracy, who were expected to take a lead both in local government and in financing building projects and civic festivals and entertainment. Agricola, for example, who became governor in AD 78 and for whom we possess a detailed biography, is said to have encouraged the building of temples, public squares and mansions, doubtless all paid for out of the private, British purse. An inscription of AD 79, recording the completion of the forum at Verulamium, might appear to confirm this although, in reality, the building was probably begun under his predecessor, Julius Frontinus.

The forum was the most important part of a Roman town, for it represented the administrative, commercial and often the religious focus. Most fora in Britain were of comparatively simple design, with a great hall, the basilica, as a place of assembly on one side, and shops and offices surrounding a square or rectangular piazza forming the other three ranges. It was here that the town council of a *civitas* – the *ordo* – would have met to sort out the levying of taxes, justice, maintenance and other local services, a task that they performed on behalf of the provincial administration. The council was normally intended to consist of some one hundred elected decurions, being men over twenty-five years of age who were owners of a not inconsiderable amount of property. They

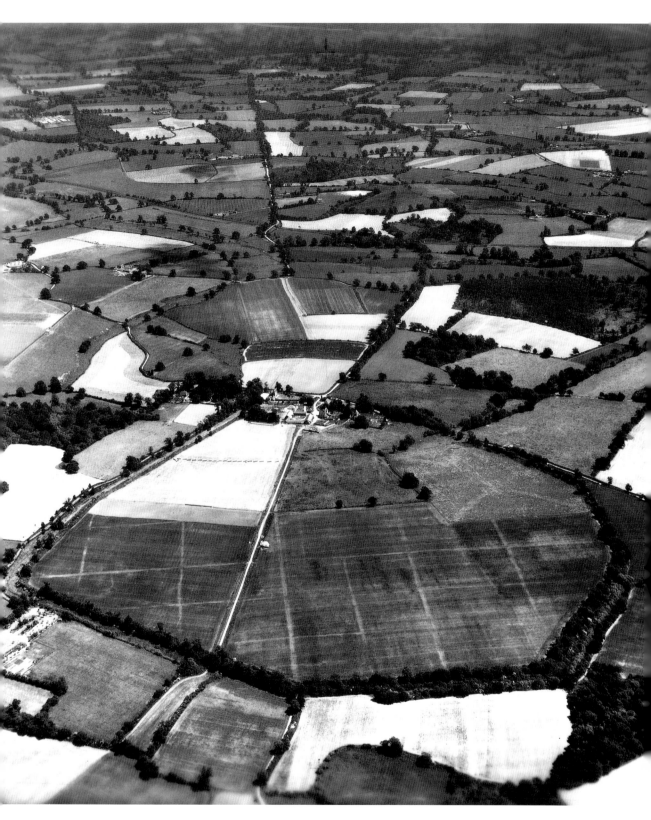

elected two senior and two junior magistrates to direct the affairs of the *civitas*, and were themselves expected to contribute personally by paying for public buildings and services. The exacting nature of this obligation may explain why most towns in Britain developed only very slowly; the wealth to pay for public monuments and comfortable private houses had to be accumulated, a process that took time, and town councils were probably well short of the desired one hundred members. Nevertheless, for those who pursued this path, a political career might develop, carrying the reward of personal advancement and prestige.

If we look at Silchester, for example, a site until recently largely studied with imperfect methods in the late nineteenth century but still the most extensively explored Romano-British town, the number of richly appointed houses is really quite small and they date mainly to the later Roman period. Indeed, even in the *coloniae*, Mediterranean styles of house do not appear until a century or more after Britain had become a Roman province. Few Britons, it would seem, ascended high on the social ladder.

What the Roman authorities probably did insist on was that the major towns, including the *civitates*, had a properly laid-out street system (including provision for drainage), dividing the town into rectangular blocks; that there was an adequate water-supply; and that amenities like public baths and lavatories were constructed. Baths, designed with warm and hot rooms, and cold plunges, were seen as an important recreational facility and as an essential facet of classical life, and made their appearance, albeit in unelaborate form, at an early stage in many towns. Indeed, by about AD 100, many of the larger settlements of the province (and these were almost exclusively confined to the south-eastern part of Britain) had acquired the main features of a Roman town. Other things came later or sometimes not at all. Whilst temples proliferated, normally in a style that blended Celtic and Roman architectural traditions, theatres (which may often have had a religious role rather than just one of entertainment), have been revealed by excavation in just three towns, and amphitheatres are known in only six or seven. Town walls, probably in some cases built more for show than for pragmatic reasons, were rare before the later second century, and British towns, although usually provided with a water-supply, lacked the great aqueducts in which large numbers of the rich Mediterranean *coloniae* and *municipia* invested so many resources. A Roman visitor to Britain, if struck by a certain lack of lavishness, would not, however, have found things too unfamiliar. He could be sure that the main public buildings existed (including an inn) and the grid of town blocks, with the forum at or near the centre, would have been an instantly recognisable pattern. Familiar too would be the rows of shops where artisans, bakers, butchers and the rest worked in open-fronted houses and lived over the premises. One has only to visit the older quarters of present-day Rome, and wander through the streets of leatherworkers or carpenters, to grasp something of the atmosphere of a Roman town of antiquity. To be sure, if our visitor came from ancient Rome itself, he might have been surprised at the open spaces, vegetable plots and orchards which seem to have been commonplace in

14 *Aerial photograph of the town of Calleva Atrebatum, modern Silchester near Reading. The grid of streets shows very clearly, as does the line of the third-century town walls, marked by trees.*

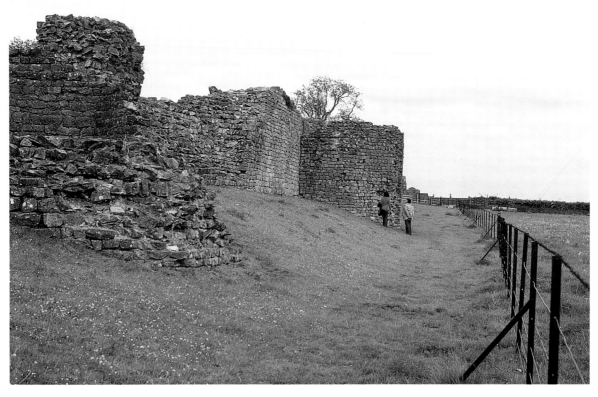

15 *The town wall of Venta Silurum, modern Caerwent (Gwent). Built about AD 300, it replaced earlier earthwork defences. The external towers, perhaps used for mounting artillery, were added around the middle of the fourth century.*

British towns; but Rome was a teeming, overcrowded city of multi-storey tenements, eighteen or more metres high (60 ft), whereas a town like Silchester can scarcely have had a population of more than a few thousand.

That the economic base of most towns was agricultural seems clear enough; they and their territories were both producers and consumers. The profit from the surplus, transported to larger market centres down an excellent road system or by boat, was invested in public or private buildings, so that a successful town like Verulamium or Cirencester could eventually boast many prestigious monuments and houses. Only in the north and west, where the military had to maintain a more or less unbroken presence for the whole of the province's history, did urbanisation really fail to take root. The forts of Vindolanda or Housesteads, with their modest civilian villages (*vici*), might be taken to epitomise the situation – a far cry, this, from the rich settlements that grew up around a north African fortress like Lambaesis. Equally, there were many small towns in the southern lowlands where an absence of a formalised street grid, a civic centre and other public buildings, betray their low rank. Some like Braughing, in Hertfordshire, were probably tolerably wealthy and a big step up from pre-Roman days; but to Roman eyes they were places of little consequence, a view coloured above all by that indulgent ethos of the ancient world that 'conspicious consumption' was everything.

We have left one highly significant town unmentioned until now, principally because it is so difficult to classify: namely London. Described by Tacitus as being, in AD 60, a town that 'was not graced with the title of *colonia*, but was an important centre for businessmen and merchandise', London may well have become the provincial capital in the years following the Iceni revolt led by Queen Boudicca. Destined to become the hub of the island's road network, the city has yielded one very precious monument: the tombstone of Classicianus. He was a Gaul who was sent to Britain as procurator – the province's finance-officer – in the aftermath of the Boudiccan revolt, and who is likely to have died while in office. An exemplary programme of excavation, carried out in hectic moments before sites are redeveloped in modern London's mad rush to change its face, has yielded much critical new evidence. Thus, we now know of an elaborate forum, first laid out in the years following the revolt, and then rebuilt, with a huge basilica, the largest in northern Europe; of a major waterfront development, datable to AD 63; of an early second-century fort at Cripplegate; and of numerous rich public and private monuments, including an amphitheatre, and large public baths. London, probably more than any other town in Britain, became a successful centre in the later first and second centuries AD, and was apparently modelled very much on Mediterranean lines. That London, like so many other urban sites selected by the Roman authorities, has, despite the vicissitudes of history, maintained that success is no mean tribute to those Roman planners. Whatever judgement we may place upon their system of values, their pragmatism, their ability in architecture and engineering and their political skills have surely stood the test of time

Chapter 4 | Villas and country estates

To an affluent Roman, the main form of investment was in land. If farmed directly, land could normally be expected to yield a profit in terms of a surplus; alternatively, it could be let out to a tenant for an agreed sum of rent or a share in the produce. In either case, misfortune apart, to be the owner of land was seen to be the most secure and socially respectable option, with the result that some of the richer families might well – and did – possess property in many different provinces of the empire. To take the emperor as an example, there were Imperial holdings in almost every province, variously acquired by confiscation, inheritance or bequest and, on occasion, by purchase. These guaranteed a very substantial income, something of great importance in the ancient world: for, without a minimum level of property, and the wealth to promote one's image, it was impossible to aspire to rank or office at either a national or a local level.

What pattern of land-owning operated in Roman Britain is very hard to say, mainly because our written sources are at best meagre. However, there is reason to think that in some respects it may have differed from that of the Mediterranean world. This we can conclude from the fact that most villas in Britain achieved a full 'Roman' style of architecture and decoration only after two or three centuries of provincial rule: that it was the fourth century AD – a time of decline in some other parts of the empire – that saw the heyday of the villa in Britain. In other words, few Romans found it desirable to buy up land in Britain in the years following the conquest.

What then was a villa? In part, it could be a country residence designed to impress. Thus in Italy we find villas such as Settefinestre, near Orbetello, to the north-west of Rome, with towers and walls imitating the defences of a town; while at the villa of Nador in coastal Algeria there is a monumental entrance with a boastful inscription, put up by an ostentatious owner for all those passing by along the main road to see. It was a matter of prestige that one's villa should be embellished with handsome mosaics on the floor (and sometimes on walls and vaults); with elaborate paintings, figured or geometric, on the walls and ceilings; and with veneers and floors made of different types of marble, imported at great expense from the Aegean, Asia Minor, Tunisia or elsewhere. One can hardly overestimate the degree of conceit and arrogance that some of these villa mansions reflect. Early examples are very rare in Britain but at Fishbourne, near Chichester in Sussex, an enormous complex of more than 4.5 hectares (10 acres) was laid out over earlier buildings about AD 75. It comprised four ranges of rooms, grouped around a formal garden, with an audience chamber, an assembly hall, a suite of baths and other private and reception areas. Extensive use was made of mosaic, painted wall-plaster and imported marble for inlaid floors, and there were some typically Italian moulded friezes in stucco. Interestingly, one recently discovered mosaic embodies a town wall, towers and gates in its design.

16 *The bust of a man, one of two heads found in a basement room at the villa at Lullingstone, Kent. Made of a Greek marble (probably Pentelic), and dating to the second century AD, they assuredly represent owners of the villa. In the fourth century they were housed beneath the Christian chapel (see illustrations 47, 79), where they remained until discovered in 1949. Height 71.1 cm (28 in).*

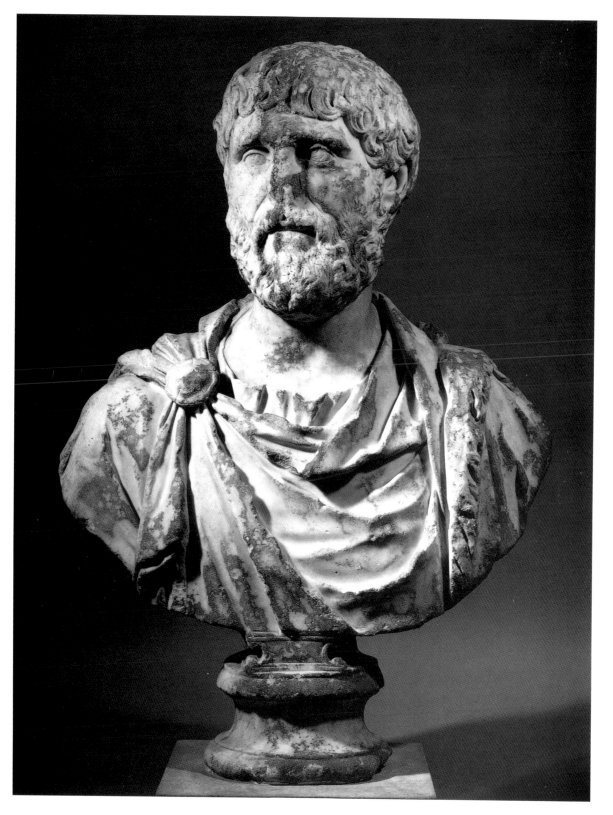

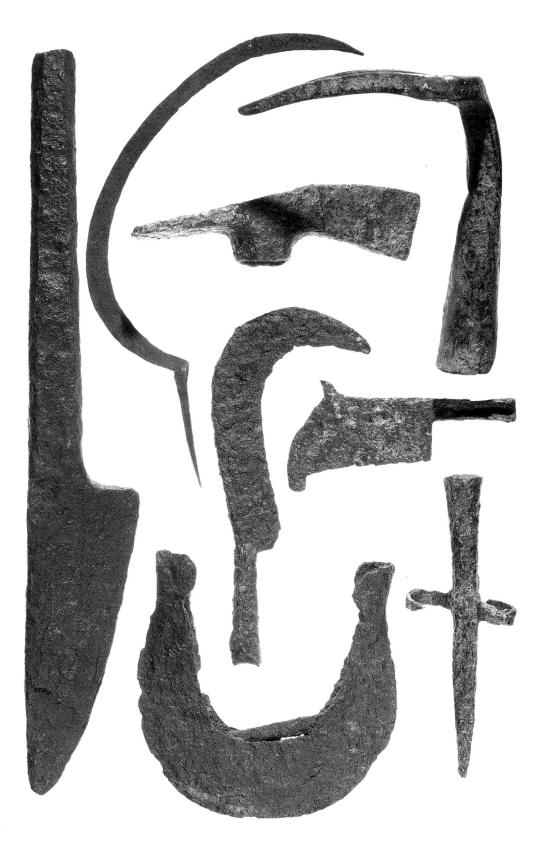

In fact, it is clear that the architect and his craftsmen were thoroughly conversant with styles and techniques of the Mediterranean world, something that is extraordinarily rare in buildings of this time in Britain. Just who the owner may have been – a rich native magnate from the local ruling family or a high-ranking Roman – is a matter for speculation; but there is no doubt that his ostentatious residence was a match for many contemporary villas in Italy or elsewhere in the Roman world.

However, it would be a mistake to imagine that a villa was just a splendid country house. As today, houses varied in size and lavishness, according to the wealth and whim of their owners; but much more importantly most villas were also the centres of farming estates. Thus, at Settefinestre, the residence lay side by side with a complex of barns, stables, a pigsty, oil and wine presses and slaves' quarters; and similarly in Britain, most villas also included working farms. We may take as an example the villa situated on the lower slopes of the chalk downland at Bignor in Sussex. The villa divides into two parts: four ranges of rooms surrounding a court measuring 61 x 35 m (200 x 115 ft) and, beyond, a walled enclosure with various farm buildings. Dating mainly to the fourth century, like most of the more elaborate villas in Britain, the rooms around the court include the residence and baths for the owner and his family, as well as service areas, a kitchen and workshops. Several of the rooms have fine mosaics, some showing figures from classical mythology, and some are provided with a hypocaust system for underfloor heating.

It is the study of the farm buildings, however, that really brings out an impression of life at Bignor in the fourth century. Without going into the calculations in detail, the size of the buildings, together with the evidence of documents and present-day agriculture, suggest that some forty to fifty labourers may have worked at Bignor on an estate of some 283 hectares (800 acres). There were probably about two hundred sheep; twelve teams of oxen for ploughing and about fifty other cattle for meat and milk; and a total yield of some 10,000 bushels (363,677 litres) of cereals, cultivated on a rotational system. This would have been enough to ensure an excellent profit for the landowner, who may well have lived for some of the time in the nearest town, Chichester, leaving a bailiff to run his affairs in the country. By way of comparison, the villa at Settefinestre is thought, on the basis of figures provided by ancient writers (several of whom produced practical manuals about agriculture), to have been an estate of some 125 hectares (300 acres) which, with fifty or so slaves, could produce a surplus of no fewer than 110,000 litres (24,200 gallons) of wine, as well as a huge quantity of cereals.

These figures are necessarily little more than educated guesswork: but they do illustrate the order of profit that a successful landowner might achieve. No wonder that some of the richest families could accumulate an annual income of over 1500 Roman pounds of gold per year, a figure equivalent to some 487 kg (1070 lb)! Not that this was the result of any miraculous, novel technology. Much of the equipment used on the farms was comparatively primitive and it seems unlikely that farming methods changed very much from those used in the Iron Age (although

17 *A group of iron agricultural tools, including a plough coulter* (*left*), *sickles, an axe, a hoe and the iron edging of a wooden shovel* (*bottom*).

there are signs of diversification of crops, and some new technology, in Britain in the fourth century). On the other hand, techniques of management probably improved sharply, in response to a series of new and enlarged markets. It has been estimated, for example, that one legion alone would consume 500 bushels (18,200 litres) of grain every week. This, combined with stable political conditions and good communications, must certainly have encouraged prosperity. If so, the farmer in Britain nevertheless acquired his wealth comparatively slowly. This much is clear from many meticulous excavations on villa sites, designed to demonstrate not just the plan of the buildings but also their history. Leaving aside those few villas, like Fishbourne, whose owners were building in the Roman manner from soon after the conquest, most villas show only a gradual adoption of classical styles. As we hinted earlier, many of these sites started life as late Iron Age farms, usually with circular wooden houses. In some more peripheral areas, such as Whitton, in south Wales, this style of round buildings persisted in use well into the second century; but in other regions, particularly south-east England, a rectilinear plan, on Roman lines, soon came into vogue.

Here, there can be little doubt that the majority of the owners were native gentry, perhaps responding to governors like Agricola who, in AD 79, encouraged the building of 'temples, public squares and private

18 A bronze statuette of a ploughman with a team of oxen found at Piercebridge, Co. Durham. It is possible that this represents a religious scene, perhaps the ploughing of the boundary marking the future line of the wall of a city. Length 7.5 cm (3 in).

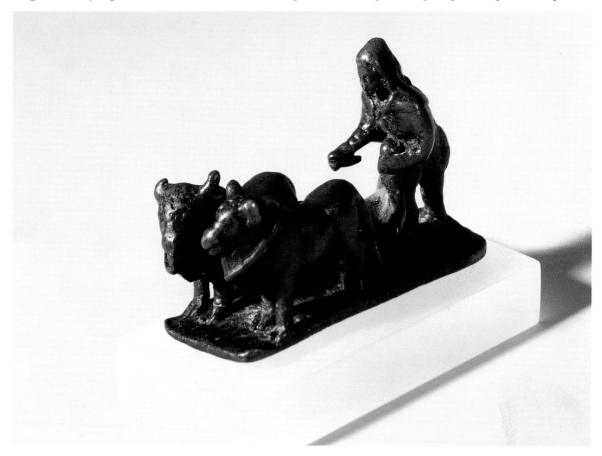

houses ... and so the Britons were gradually led on to the amenities that make vice agreeable – arcades, baths and sumptuous banquets.'

Despite this official encouragement (and the option of borrowing money to develop one's property), the fact of the matter is that some villa owners achieved success, while many others did not. Thus, at Gadebridge Park, not far from Verulamium, the owner started with a timber house and a small bath-suite, built about AD 75; subsequently the property was gradually expanded, so that by the early fourth century, there was both a handsome residence and a complex of associated buildings. Even a large swimming pool was attached to the baths (possibly more for public than for private use). At Whitton, on the other hand, the occupants never achieved more than some rectangular buildings with stone footings, two hypocausts that were never fired and a very small quantity of painted wall-plaster. Much of the reason may have been geographical. It is a conspicuous feature of the distribution of 'successful' villas that the majority cluster around the towns of southern England. These provided market outlets and an urban residence for those owners who preferred, like so many Romans, to leave their country estate (or estates) in the hands of bailiffs. In the north and west, however, not only were towns much less common but there was a continual need for an army of occupation, hardly ideal conditions for the accumulation of much private wealth. Northern villas there were, some possibly owned by retired army veterans – but they are neither common nor particularly rich. Nevertheless, as a whole, the villa-system did work in Britain. Many Britons became Romanised, they farmed profitably and they flourished at a time when a considerable number of other provinces witnessed a gradual but widespread desertion of the land. A British villa owner might well have been proud when, in AD 359, the emperor Julian, faced with a crisis, was able to increase the regular shipment of grain from Britain to the Rhineland by no less than 600 bargeloads. It is no small measure of the province's agricultural success.

To these remarks we must add an important postscript. It would be all too easy to imagine that south-east England in particular was farmed more or less exclusively by villa estates; but this would be a quite erroneous picture. Side by side with the villas were very large numbers of more Iron Age style settlements, taking up more than 90 per cent of the landscape and many of them originating well before the conquest. Here were people whose aspirations to become 'Roman' were much less, although many may have worked on the villa estates in addition to tending their own land. One region of native-style settlement is particularly thoroughly documented, the East Anglian Fenland, and it is to a brief survey of that area that we shall now turn.

Chapter 5 | A Roman landscape: the East Anglian Fenland

Stretching northwards from the city of Cambridge lies Britain's largest area of flat-lands, the Fens. Once a vast basin hollowed out by the sea, this low-lying terrain is made up of an intricate blend of marine and fresh-water flood deposits which have created so level a plain that in places one can even detect the curvature of the earth. Only a few small 'islands' of higher and older ground – now mostly occupied by towns and villages – break up the monotony of a vista otherwise taken up with unending fields of arable.

From the air, however, this landscape acquires a quite new meaning. Mapped out with extraordinary clarity by colour changes in the soil and by different levels of growth in the crops are the courses of long-extinct rivers and streams, Roman drove-roads, canals and field-systems; Romano-British villages and farms where even individual houses can sometimes be picked out; and the many traces of still older activity such as the ditches of Bronze Age burial mounds. Archaeological investigation of these features has shown them to result from a complex series of episodes in the history of the landscape. During the Iron Age, the coast lay 24 km (15 miles) or more south of its present position, fringing a huge wet peat bog. Only the islands of higher ground were open to settlement, and it is now known that they were extensively occupied by communities exploiting the rich and varied resources of a marshland environment. One such place was Stonea, near the modern town of March, where a site (Stonea 'Camp') enclosed by a bank and ditch, and surrounded by dense oak forest, came into being in the course of the second century BC. Dismembered human remains from the ditch suggest some arcane ritual purpose, probably as a ceremonial centre for a western enclave of the Iceni tribe. Later, it may have been the place to which the Iceni retreated in AD 47, after a revolt, only to be thrashed by the Roman army; but, whatever the truth of that, there can be no doubt that the unsuccessful rebellion of AD 60-61, led by Queen Boudicca, had grave repercussions for the area. This is evident from the large number of hoards of silver and gold Iceni coins that were buried for safety at this time at Stonea and its vicinity. One, found in 1982 at Field Baulk, March, consisted of a globular pot containing no fewer than 872 silver coins of typical dish-shaped form, which had been concealed in a pit. It is the largest hoard of Iceni coins yet known.

It is also around this time that changes in land and sea levels brought about drastic alterations to the Fens. The sea receded, allowing the silts it had laid down to dry out, and the marshes to the south slowly turned into semi-arid peat. Gradually, the newly available silt lands (although not the unstable peats) were colonised. The first settlers were mainly salters, whose sites are easily recognised from the fired clay kiln furniture (briquetage) used to support the brine container while it was

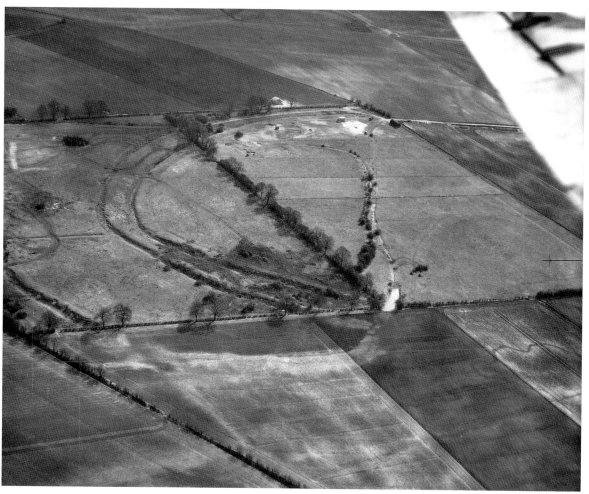

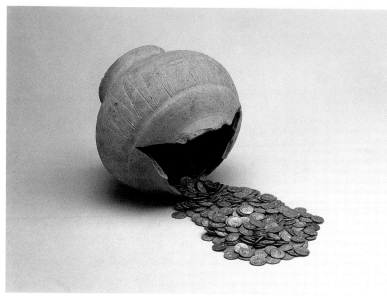

19 *Aerial photograph of Stonea Camp, showing the ramparts. A centre of the Iceni tribe, at its maximum it covered 8 hectares (19.8 acres). It was founded in the second century* BC, *probably for religious and commercial purposes, rather than as a settlement, and remained in use until the time of Boudicca's revolt.*

20 *Some of the 872 Iceni silver coins, and their pottery container, found at Field Baulk, March, Cambridgeshire in 1982. This very large hoard was probably concealed during the troubled times of the Boudiccan revolt of* AD 60-61.

21 *Part of a Romano-British village at Grandford, near March, Cambridgeshire, photographed from the air while under grass. Probably originating as a Roman fort, established in the aftermath of the Boudiccan revolt, there can be seen the ditches demarcating fields (left), flanked by a road, the Fen Causeway, as well as house enclosures.*

slowly heated. Then, around AD 120-40, the picture changed dramatically. Hundreds of villages and farms were founded all over the northern Fenland and also on the stable ground of the islands in the south. Typified by wooden cottages with thatched roofs, set within rectangular enclosures formed by drainage ditches, the buildings are not those of villa-owners, however; rather, they are the very modest dwellings of peasants, living at a low level of subsistence and with comparatively few possessions of any quality. Moreover, study of the animal bones suggests that the main activity was not the cultivation of cereals (as it is today) but the raising of sheep for wool, and the salting of meat.

Many believe that they can detect signs of the hand of government in this massive increase in the population of the Fenland: that this was state-owned land (acquired by confiscation after Boudicca's revolt)

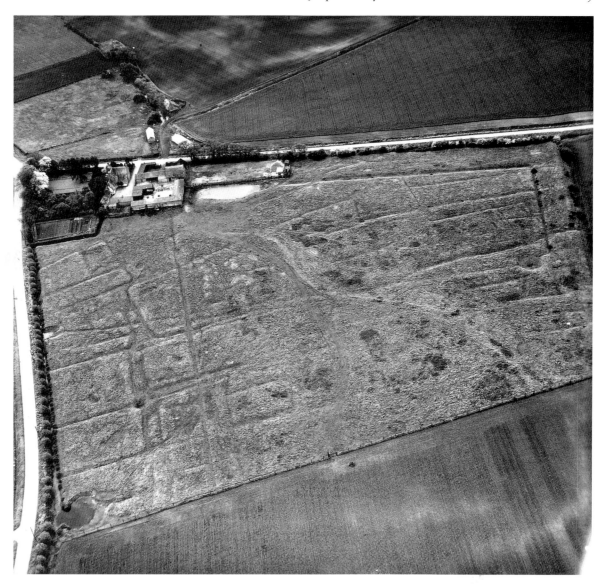

farmed in the main by tenants, and it is a view that finds support in the fact that, so far as we can tell, a number of drainage canals and carefully laid-out roads were constructed at about the same time. These massive works of civil engineering were clearly the result not of private but of public enterprise; and the same must be true of a major site, excavated by the British Museum, at Stonea.

Situated close to the old Iceni centre of Stonea Camp, probably for symbolic reasons, the site turned out to comprise a very large and imposing complex, set out in a carefully planned and organised way. Its central feature was a stone building, which may have risen several storeys, a typical example of Roman 'prestige' architecture. As there is no stone in the Fens, all the building materials had to be brought from the Peterborough area, some 48 km (30 miles) away, and the structure was handsomely embellished with mosaic, finely painted wall-plaster and glazed windows. Under-floor heating was provided and the roof covered with tiles. In front was an extensive piazza, running up to a wide gravel-metalled road, the main artery of the settlement. To one side was a compound, divided up into blocks by a grid of streets. Each block contained a number of relatively simple wooden houses, together with wells, latrines and carefully organised areas of refuse pits. On the other side of the main road, a street led to a fairly elaborate stone temple, with a façade formed by two rows of wooden columns; the finds, especially of figurines, suggest that it was probably dedicated to Minerva, one of the three state divinities of Rome.

22 Reconstruction of what the settlement at Stonea could have looked like in the second century. In front of the stone building is a large piazza, here interpreted as a market, with domestic housing beyond.

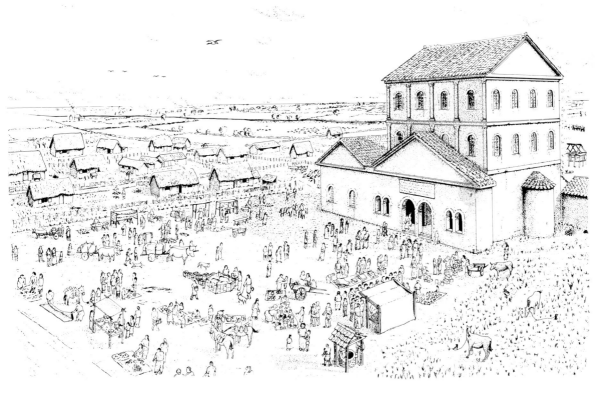

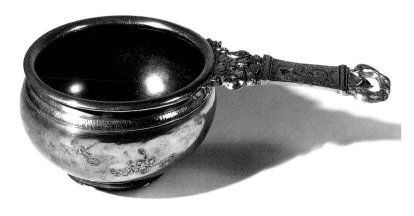

23 *An exceptionally fine bronze saucepan or skillet, with a highly decorated inlaid handle bearing the maker's name, Boduogenus. Second century AD. Found at Prickwillow near Ely in the Fenland.*

It is clear from study of the pottery and coins that the site was laid out during Hadrian's reign (AD 117-38), and is thus contemporary with the development of the Fens as a whole. Moreover, items of military equipment indicate that a number of soldiers were present, probably to administer the region. Still more remarkably, examination of the animal bones indicate that the principal activity was the export of joints of salted meat, especially lamb. The provision of meat both for the army and for officials was one of the duties of the State, and the evidence from the settlement at Stonea suggests this was its principal role. But it will surely also have acted as a political and judicial centre, doubtless focused upon the great stone building. Tantalisingly, it is still not possible to decipher the words scratched upon the several wooden writing tablets that were found; here may lie further clues as to the site's role in the region.

In the apparent absence of other conventional amenities of Roman settlements, such as baths, life at Stonea can hardly, however, have been congenial. Some wine and olive oil, and luxuries such as figs, did reach its occupants from time to time, as pottery containers and the plant remains show: but Stonea (whose Roman name is alas still unknown) was not destined to grow into the civilised place that its founders may have wanted.

24 *Some of the pottery vessels cast into a ditch as the Romans cleaned out their stores when demolishing the stone-built complex at Stonea about AD 200. They include a red-ware samian dish from Gaul, relief-decorated vessels from the Nene Valley near Peterborough and cooking pots.*

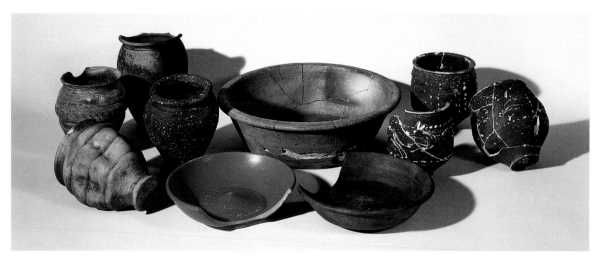

Private investment, a vital factor in the development of towns in virtually every part of the Roman empire, was conspicuously lacking. About
AD 200, the decision was taken to pull down the stone building, and
empty the official stores: scores of complete pots, with just very slight
damage, were discarded in the process, and dumped in ditches and pits.
Even so, later Roman items of military apparel suggest that a caucus of
officials remained, and the export of salted meat certainly continued,
apparently down until the abandonment of the province in the early fifth

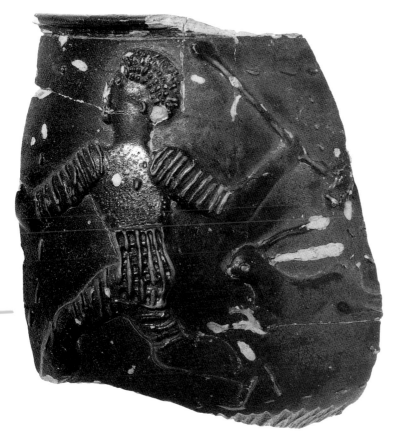

25 *Part of a colour-coated beaker,
made in the Nene Valley near
Peterborough, and found at Stonea.
An enigmatic figure, wearing
protective clothing except on his chest,
clasps a long-handled hammer, and is
accompanied by a hare. The style is
typical of Romano-British figurative
art. Late second century AD.*

century. Likewise, items of military equipment found by detectorists at
Grandford, a large Romano-British village some 9 km (5½ miles) to the
north-west of Stonea, may indicate that the State also exercised control
in other Fenland centres. This new insight into how the Romans may
have arranged aspects of their economy is particularly intriguing, and is
matched by the recent discovery of a large stone-built barn, in the heart
of another extensive Romano-British settlement near Chatteris. Despite
the massive damage inflicted upon the archaeological remains of the
Fenland by modern agriculture, there are evidently many more novelties
to be brought to light. It is a reminder that our understanding of the
past is never static, but rather a constant reassessment as new evidence
and new ideas are brought into play.

Chapter 6 | The Roman army

One of the major achievements of the Romans was the development of a highly efficient, professional army. In open battle, few forces could withstand so organised and skilful a body, and the pages of the ancient historians are full of stories of military valour and success. In Britain, the army played a particularly important role, both in the process of conquest and in the maintenance of peace and order. That said, it should be remembered that, in the course of time, the nature and structure of the army changed a good deal. The Roman authorities were constantly evolving new methods of warfare, and thus the army that invaded Britain in AD 43 was very different from that of the third and fourth centuries. This development can be vividly illustrated by archaeology, whether through excavation of the military bases or by study of the equipment and of contemporary representations of the soldiers on tombstones and other monuments. To these can now be added some 250 substantial texts of letters and other documents written

26 A scene from the victory column erected by the emperor Trajan (AD 98-117) in his forum in Rome. It shows legionary and auxiliary infantry engaging native troops from Dacia – modern Romania – in pitched battle. Trajan fought two wars in Dacia between 101 and 106, although some now think that the reliefs were carved at the behest of his successor, Hadrian.

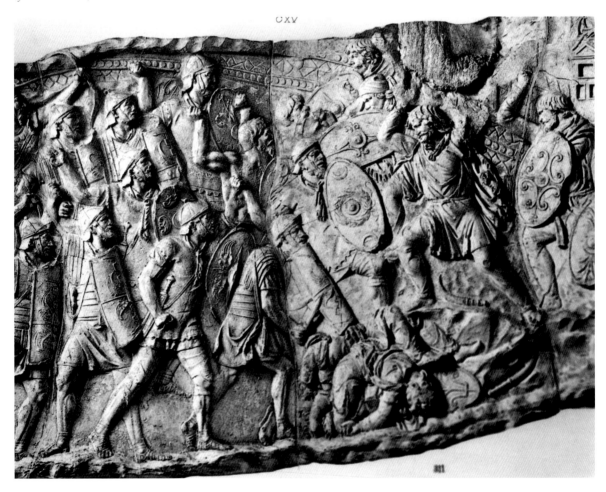

in ink upon wooden writing tablets from the fort of Vindolanda, near Hadrian's Wall. These shed unique light upon life on a Roman frontier between about AD 90 to 120.

It was the legions that formed the core of the Roman army. Numbering some twenty-five in the first century AD, these were units of heavily armed infantry each consisting of some 5000 men. Every man had to be a Roman citizen, an indication of the high social status of the force. In command of each legion was a legate, a man of senatorial rank, often part-way through an illustrious political career. The future emperor, Vespasian, for instance, was in charge of the IInd Augusta legion during the early days of the conquest of Britain. The post of legate was thus a very senior one, whose appointment lay in the hands of the emperor himself. However, while many legates may have served as junior officers, prowess in military affairs was by no means the sole qualification for the job. Although connections in high places were always helpful in gaining advancement, it was expected that a legate should be an accomplished administrator, whose role could well involve him in civilian as well as in military matters. This must have been particularly the case in a province like Britain, where the army supervised an area with very few towns. To aid him, the legate had six junior officers, called tribunes, and, as a direct link between him and his men, a hierarchy of sixty centurions. These were the most experienced soldiers in the legion, each leading a 'century' of eighty men; many a battle was won because of the centurions' know-how and skill. Promotion to this post, the dream of most legionaries, could take years; but it brought its rewards, not least a pay-packet twenty times as great as that of an ordinary legionary.

The legionary soldier himself was normally recruited between the ages of eighteen to twenty, to serve for a period of twenty-five years. He was expected to be very fit and, if possible, from a suitable background. As Vegetius, the author of a late-Roman military manual, remarks: 'Smiths, blacksmiths, wagon-makers, butchers and huntsmen, whether of stag or boar, are fitted for association with the services ... fishermen, fowlers, confectioners and weavers ... should not, in my opinion, be allowed near the barracks.' During the first century AD, the majority of legionaries were drawn from Italy, southern France and southern Spain; but, in the course of the second century, grants of citizenship brought in a great influx of legionaries from north Africa and the Danube provinces. Although it was a very hard, disciplined life, the excellent prospects for promotion and the enticement of a large pension grant, in land or in cash, ensured a constant supply of new recruits. The legionaries were undoubtedly the backbone of the Roman structure of empire.

The rest of the army was made up of units of auxiliary troops, *auxilia*, which literally means 'aids'. However, they were not just supplementary forces. Unlike legionaries, they did not have to be Roman citizens, and they were generally raised in newly acquired provinces. This sometimes resulted in the recruitment of specialist soldiers, like units of archers from Syria, who are readily identifiable by their characteristic bow, arrows, axe and conical helmet. But, more usually, the auxiliaries fitted into a fairly standard pattern of organisation. Their regiments consisted both of infantry and cavalry, normally numbering some 480 men. The infantry were the more common and the cavalry more prestigious. This was because the legions were comparatively weak in mounted troops, and the auxiliary cavalry were thus in demand to guard the flanks; as a consequence they came to be known as *alae*, from the Latin word ala, a wing. In addition, there were also units which combined both infantry and cavalry. These highly mobile and flexible regiments could deal with a great variety of tasks and became increasingly common; indeed, by Hadrian's day, about AD 120, over half the auxiliary units in Britain were mixed, part of a force which probably numbered altogether some 35,000 men.

27 *Part of the wooden tablet from Vindolanda listing the strength of the First Cohort of Tungrians, under the command of Julius Verecundus. It dates to c. AD 92-7.*

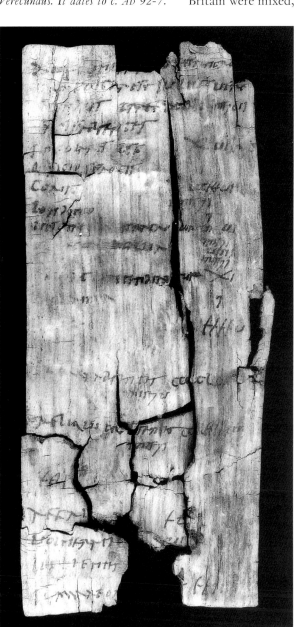

Particular light is cast on this by a 'strength report' from Vindolanda. This reveals that the unit, the First Cohort of Tungrians (raised in what is now southern Belgium) had a total complement of 752 men. However, no fewer than 456 are listed as being on detached duty, in seven different places, one being London. Of the remaining soldiers, fifteen are described as sick, six as wounded and ten as suffering from inflammation of the eyes. Flexibility in the composition, and disposition, of army units, as need arose, was clearly the norm. Not that the Britons seemed to pose much threat at the time: as an intelligence report observes, 'the Britons are unprotected by armour. There are very many cavalry. The cavalry do not use swords nor do the *Brittunculi* ('wretched little Brits') mount in order to throw javelins'.

The auxiliary regiments were led by an officer of equestrian rank, who was often, like his men, of provincial origin; the Tungrians at Vindolanda were for example commanded by a man called Julius Verecundus, himself probably a Tungrian. As with the legate of a legion, this was usually a step in his career, so that those who were a success might progress to the post of junior tribune in a legion or to command one of the few double-size cavalry regiments, before returning to senior civilian appointments. Below him in the chain of command were either centurions (in the infantry units) or decurions (for the cavalry), so that the overall structure bore many points of resemblance to that of the legions. As far as the men were concerned, there seems never to have been a shortage of volunteers, at any rate in the days of the early empire. The great incentive was the grant of citizenship and right to marry which the auxiliary soldier received at the end of his twenty-five years' service. Until the early third century, when citizenship was extended to all free-born inhabitants of the empire, this allowed a soldier to raise both his own status and that of his wife and children to a very considerable degree – something of immense importance in a world preoccupied with questions of rank and prestige.

Archaeological evidence has a good deal to tell us about the equipment of the Roman army, partly through illustrations on stone or metal but also from the objects themselves. Weapons were subject to tight controls and, although paid for by the individual soldiers when issued from the stores, had to be surrendered upon discharge from the army (presumably with a refund) – a sensible measure, designed to prevent swords and the like getting into the wrong hands. Legionary issue was in fact very standardised. Each soldier carried two javelins which would be thrown at the beginning of an engagement with the intention of impaling and thus rendering useless the shields of the enemy. The famed short, broad-bladed sword, the *gladius*, could then be employed to deadly effect in the press of fighting at close quarters. A dagger (carried by most legionaries until it became unfashionable about AD 100) might also be used, although most examples known to us seem to be more items of display than for fighting.

Protective armour was more varied and altered considerably during Roman times: but a soldier of the later first and second centuries AD would probably have been dressed in a light suit of overlapping iron strips, giving him considerable freedom of movement. His officers would have been easily recognisable by their sheet metal breast plates and decorated shin-guards or by their elegant scale-armour, sewn onto a tunic of leather or linen. Both would have worn helmets (whose form changed considerably over the centuries) and carried a curved rectangular shield, made of plywood covered with goatskin; only the edge-binding, hand-grip and central boss were of metal. The auxiliary infantryman, on the other hand, had a simple spear in place of the javelin, although his sword was

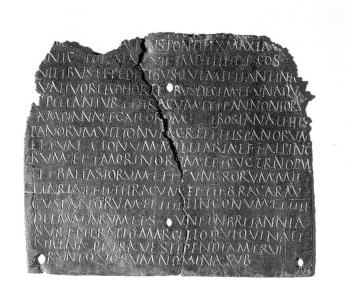

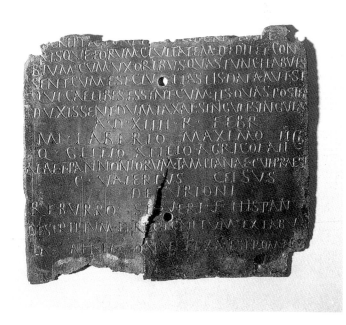

28 *A bronze diploma found at Malpas, Cheshire. It conferred the rights of citizenship and of marriage upon a Spaniard, Reburrus, after twenty-five years' service, which led to his becoming a cavalry officer. It is dated to AD 103. 15.6 x 12.7 cm, 15.6 x 1.33 cm (6.1 x 5 in, 6.1 x 5.2 in).*

29 *A legionary helmet in bronze, and a shield boss, with the names of their owners punched onto them. Decorative motifs on the shield boss include the four seasons, legionary standards and a bull (the symbol of the VIIIth legion, in which its owner, Iunius Dubitatus, served). From the Rivers Thames and Tyne.*

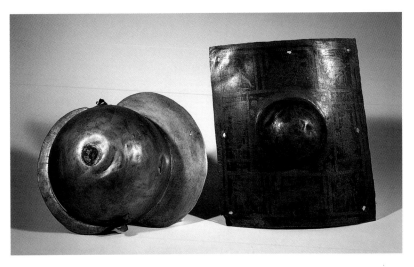

much the same as that of the legionary. Helmet types differed slightly, and his shield was oval and flat, while the armour consisted of a mail shirt, of small interconnecting iron rings. Below that were knee-length trousers, perhaps made of leather, a sharp contrast from the skirt-like tunic generally worn by legionary soldiers in all but very cold climates.

The equipment and dress of cavalrymen was slightly modified so as to take account of their rather different role in battle; but, in overall terms, it is remarkable to see how standardised the Roman army became

30 *A group of legionary weapons of the first century AD, with javelin heads, a dagger and a sword and their sheaths. From the fort at Hod Hill, Dorset, except for the sword, which was found in the River Thames at Fulham, London.*

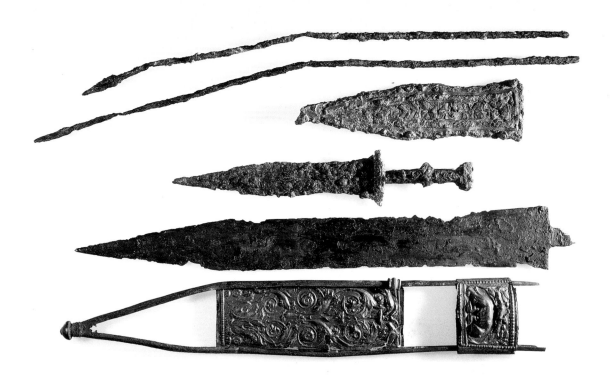

in its dress and armour. Similarly, the layout of the auxiliary forts and the legionary fortresses was also to achieve a considerable degree of uniformity. In the early days of Roman expansion, in the centuries before Christ, the army normally wintered in a convenient town, taking over such accommodation as was necessary. By the time of the conquest of Britain (like much of northern Europe, a land with no proper urban centres), it was becoming customary to construct forts with ramparts of turf and regularly laid-out wooden buildings. This was not only a quick

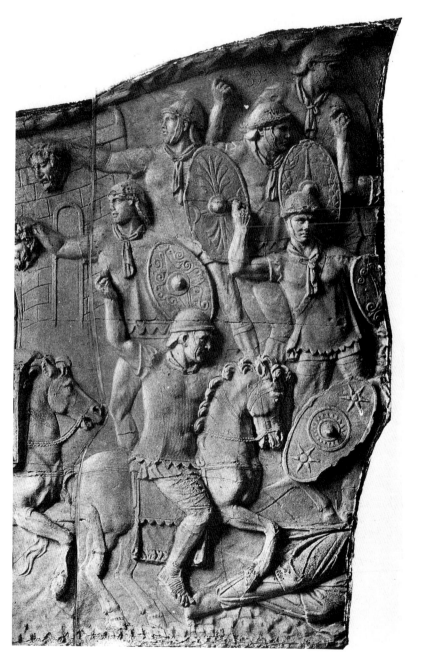

31 *A scene from Trajan's column in Rome, showing an auxiliary cavalryman in battle. He wears a mail tunic and leather trousers.*

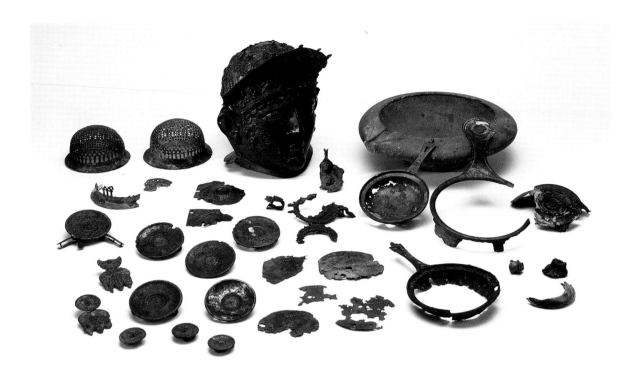

32 A hoard mainly of parade equipment of a cavalry trooper of the Ala II Asturum, based at Bremetenacum, modern Ribchester (Lancashire), where it was found in 1796. Buried in the earlier part of the second century, it includes the famous helmet, harness fittings, military awards and vessels.

and convenient method of housing the troops, but it was also an indication of the need for more permanent bases – and of the way in which the army was becoming increasingly professional. By about AD 100, when it was fairly clear that a province such as Britain would require a standing garrison, many of the military bases were rebuilt in stone, on lines that can be paralleled in most parts of the empire.

The plan of a fort or fortress was generally rectangular, with the proportions resembling those of a modern playing-card. Surrounded by ditches and a rampart or wall, the area within the defences was divided up into blocks by a grid of streets. The headquarters building lay at the centre, at the intersection of two main thoroughfares. Behind or adjacent was the commanding officer's residence, normally constructed in Italianate style, while in a legionary fortress there would be a row of houses for the senior officers, lining the main street. Other key buildings included the bath-house which, because it could be a fire hazard, was normally placed outside the defences; the granaries, where military regulations insisted that a year's supply of grain be stored; and in all fortresses and some forts a hospital. Other storage facilities and workshops apart, the remaining space was taken up with barracks and, in cavalry forts, stables.

The barracks were constructed so as to accommodate a 'century' of eighty soldiers. At one end were the centurion's quarters, while platoons of eight men were expected to share two rooms, one for living and sleeping and the other for the storage of equipment. Guard duties will have prevented all eight men being in barracks at one time but, even so, it must have been a cramped existence. Moreover, there was no centralised

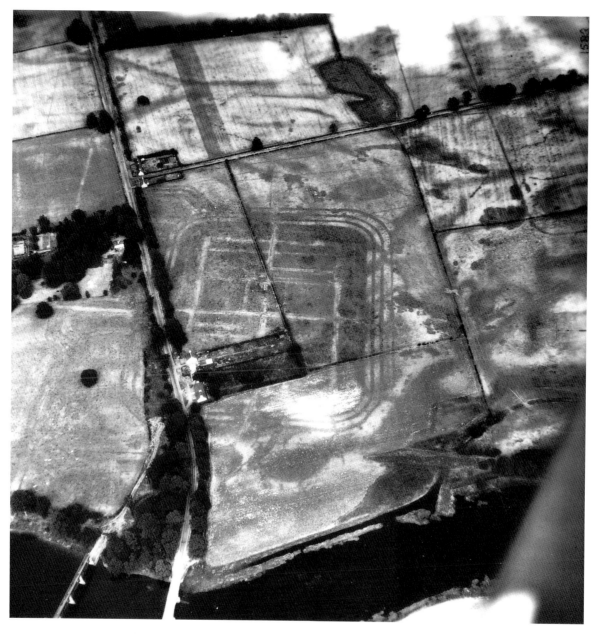

mess, so the soldiers also ate in their quarters, preparing their meals in ovens, set into the rear of the defences. Corn – which could be made not just into bread but also into porridge or pasta – bacon, cheese, salt, beer and sour wine were the staple foods, for the simple but important reason that they were unlikely ever to cause food-poisoning. Nonetheless, the importance of a balanced diet was appreciated and, whenever possible, a wide range of fruit, vegetables and animal products was also provided. This much is clear from the lists of supplies recorded on some of the Vindolanda tablets, which reveal a varied and sophisticated diet, especially for the officers: roe deer, venison, chicken, radishes, plums, pigs'

33 *Aerial view of the auxiliary fort at Glenlochar, Dumfries and Galloway. The visible remains, which include triple ditches and internal streets, date mainly to the second century.*

51

trotters, fish sauce, oysters and even pepper (a rare and expensive luxury) are amongst the items listed.

So far, we have been describing an army as it would have been known to someone serving in it in the late first or early second centuries AD. But by the days of Trajan or Hadrian, i.e. from AD 97-138, marked changes were already afoot. The empire had almost reached its period of maximum growth and the major concern lay more with the retention than the expansion of the imperial lands. Military positions were in effect fossilised so that auxiliary units were used increasingly for routine patrolling, legions for the occasional punitive campaign. Auxiliary regiments were rarely moved far from their forts, and hardly ever to another province. So it was that a new type of unit, the *numerus*, evolved. Recruited from non-citizens, they were irregular troops equipped in their native style and commanded by their own officers. They seem to

34 Bronze figurine of the healing god, Aesculapius (the Greek Asklepios) discovered near Chichester, Sussex. Although the army in particular paid great attention to medical matters, resort to healing deities was also commonplace in the ancient world; this however is the first image of Aesculapius to be found in Britain. Height 6.4 cm (2.5 in).

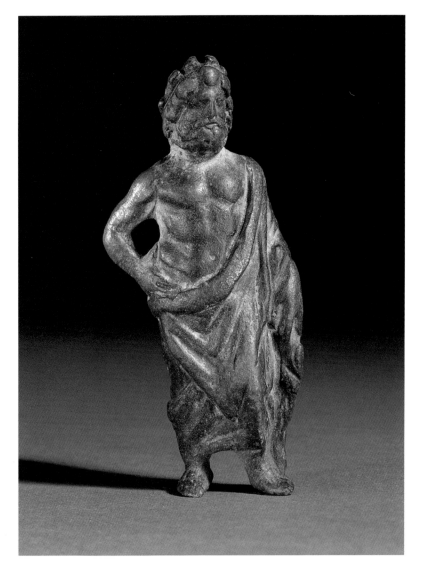

have had the mobility of the early auxiliary regiments and were often deployed on the frontiers of the empire. Similarly, the distinction between legionary and auxiliary became increasingly less marked, particularly when citizenship was granted to all the free-born in the early third century.

As a result, army life became ever less attractive. Just as in the towns councillors were unable to resign their onerous and often ruinous offices, and in the country agricultural workers became more and more tied to the land, so too a soldier's post was made hereditary and compulsory. This may not have caused great problems in Britain where the majority of soldiers' sons seem to have entered their father's unit by choice: after all, they were now allowed to marry and had a secure job. Nevertheless, army life in the late-Roman period was very different to that of before. By the early fourth century, military and civilian commands had been separated, the top army officers now being styled dukes and counts. The legions, already much shrunk in size, were split up into smaller units of about one thousand men and were supplemented by units of *equites* (cavalry) and *milites* (infantry), who were the new crack troops. In late-fourth century Britain, as is recorded in a near-contemporary document, the *Notitia Dignitatum*, there were four senior officials, of whom three were military. A count probably had a small mobile field army at his disposal, while a duke and a second count were responsible for the defence, respectively, of northern Britain and of a chain of defences around the south-east coast of England, the 'Saxon-Shore' forts. In our days of profound military change, it is a reminder that the role of an army can never be static: like any force, the Roman army did its best to adapt to circumstances. That it remained so effective for so long is a tribute to those who shaped its development.

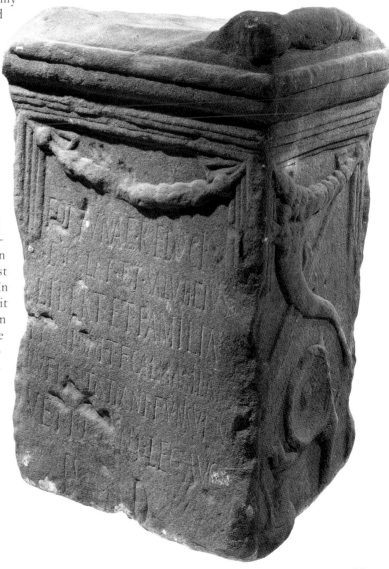

35 *An altar from the legionary fortress at Deva (modern Chester), dedicated to 'Fortune the Home-bringer, to Aesculapius and to Salus' (also a god of health) by the freedmen and slaves of the legion's legate (commander), Pomponius Mamilianus; he was doubtless in poor health. Height 73.6 cm (29.9 in).*

Chapter 7 | The frontiers of northern Britain: the second and third centuries

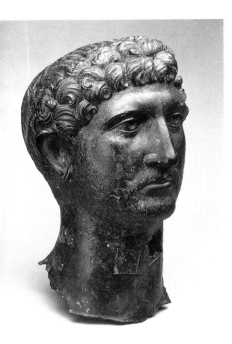

To many people, Roman Britain is synonymous with that justly famous monument, Hadrian's Wall. Stretching for 80 Roman miles (120 km, 76 miles), from the Solway Firth to the River Tyne at Wallsend, its sheer size and grandeur of design mark it out as one of the great engineering achievements of antiquity. Yet it is important to remember that, to Roman eyes, the notion that the empire should possess finite boundaries was for many centuries all but inconceivable. Only a series of grave military reverses, particularly in troublesome areas like the territory of the Germans to the east of the Rhine, brought about a change in attitude. By the 80s of the first century AD the first tentative moves were being made, both in Germany and in Scotland, to create some sort of boundary. At first these consisted of no more than a line of forts; however, within a short space of time, wooden watchtowers, linked by a patrol road, were under construction. It was the beginning of a decisive change in policy, from expansion to retrenchment, which was to have profound consequences throughout the Roman world.

As we saw earlier, Roman control of lowland Scotland did not last long. Conquered by Agricola's army in the early 80s, Scotland was soon abandoned in favour of a northern boundary between the Solway and the Tyne. Initially this consisted of no more than a road, the Stanegate, gar-

36 *Bronze head from a colossal statue (one and a quarter times life-size) of the emperor Hadrian (AD 117-138). Found in the River Thames at London Bridge, it probably stood in a public building or space such as the forum.*

37 *Hadrian's Wall and milecastle 42 at Cawfields, to the west of Housesteads. To the right are the linear banks and ditch known as the Vallum; it may have demarcated the military zone.*

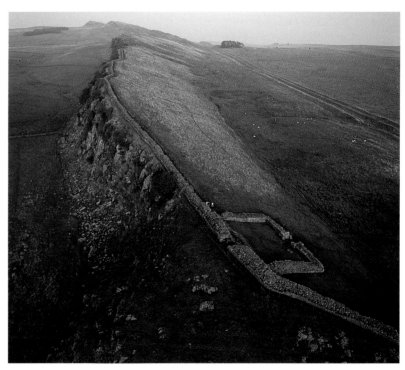

risoned by a series of auxiliary forts and by some watchtowers. However, Hadrian's visit to the province, in AD 122, changed all that. In the words of his biographer, he 'instituted many reforms and was the first to build a wall, 80 miles long, to separate the barbarians from the Romans'. Much of this highly impressive monument still survives and has been the subject of detailed and painstaking investigations. These have disclosed a long and complex history, although there are many questions that still remain unresolved.

The original plan was for a barrier that ran from a bridge over the River Tyne at Newcastle to the present-day village of Bowness, on the southern side of the Solway estuary. As far as the valley of the River Irthing, 45 Roman miles (66.6 km, 41.4 miles), the Wall was built of stone. It was at first intended that these footings should be ten Roman feet wide but this figure was subsequently reduced to eight. West of the River Irthing, at about which point the limestone ceases, the building-material was changed from stone to turf, so that the final thirty-one Roman miles consisted of a great rampart of turf blocks; later, this was replaced by a wall in stone. Wherever possible a substantial ditch was dug on the north side of the Wall, a plan abandoned only where the line ran along the crest of a cliff or where the rock was too hard to complete the job (as at Limestone Corner, where blocks of stone, one once weighing as much as 13,200 kg [13 tons], still lie scattered around). To garrison the Wall, the original blue-print was for a series of small fortlets, placed every Roman mile (1481 m, 1620 yds; hence the term 'milecastles'), with between them two regularly spaced towers or 'turrets'. Built of masonry in the eastern 'stone sector' and of wood and turf to the west, the milecastles contained units varying from about eight to sixty-four men. They are likely to have provided look-outs for the turrets (all of which were built in stone), although it was clearly envisaged that the main garrison and support troops should come from the forts a few miles behind the Wall on the Stanegate.

This scheme was soon abandoned, however, and it was decided to add a total of sixteen auxiliary forts to the frontier-line. At the same time, the decision was reached to extend the eastern end of the Wall for a further four Roman miles as far as Wallsend. The forts followed the normal layout, as we have described earlier, although there is some diversity in their relationship with the Wall; some project forward of it, others incorporate the Wall as their northern side, and a few lie to the south. The largest was at Stanwix, overlooking the Eden valley corridor, on the north-east side of Carlisle; it was probably the command centre for a force that altogether must have totalled approximately nine thousand men. Moreover there was a further defensive curtain which extend-

38 *A stone relief from the fort of Benwell on Hadrian's Wall. It records building work by the IInd Augusta legion, whose badges, the goat and Pegasus, and its standard, are shown. Length 38 cm (15 in).*

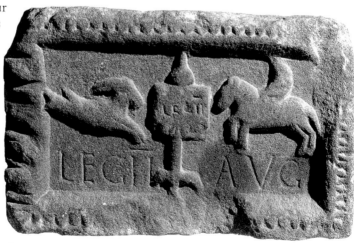

ed beyond the point where the Wall stopped in the west, at Bowness-on-Solway. From here on, much of the coastline is made up of low-lying beaches, which are particularly vulnerable to sea-borne attack from south-west Scotland. For this reason, the Roman authorities decided to build a series of fortlets and towers identically arranged to those on the Wall itself. These have been identified for a distance of some 40 km (25 miles), beyond which were Hadrianic auxiliary forts at Maryport and Ravenglass. It was certainly a frontier on an impressive scale, the more so

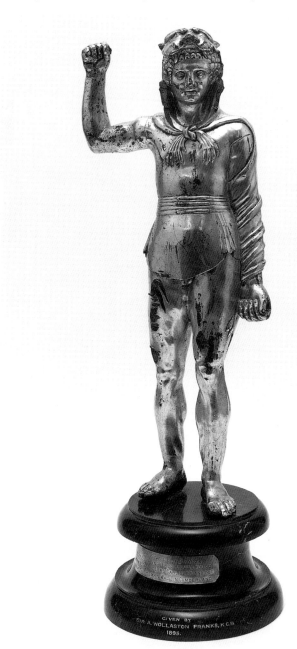

39 A gilt-bronze figure of the god Hercules, perhaps wearing a lion-skin. Found near Birdoswald fort on Hadrian's Wall, it probably comes from a military shrine. Height 50 cm (1 ft 8 in).

since recent work hints that there was probably a single or double wooden palisade linking the towers and fortlets.

Although the garrison of the frontier was made up of regiments of auxiliary soldiers, building inscriptions make it quite clear that it was the legionaries who built it – the IInd Augusta from their base at Caerleon in south Wales, the XXth Valeria Victrix from Chester in north Wales and the VIth Victrix, who came over from Germany. The governor who was initially responsible, Aulus Platorius Nepos, also came from Germany, but work on the frontier was in progress long after his departure – probably well into the 130s.

What then was its function? In part it formed a military zone, a point underlined by a ditch with mounds on either side, known today as the Vallum, which demarcates the southern perimeter of the main curtain. Crossing-points were rigorously controlled, with most traffic being channelled through rear and front gates in selected milecastles; trade and political contact beyond the frontier could thus be regulated, customs duties extracted and the export or import of illegal items such as weapons prohibited. There were also gates on the two main northern roads, whose routes were further guarded by outpost forts. These forts will also have been useful as sources of intelligence in the event of unrest, so that an army could be rapidly deployed to deal with any problem: for the design of the curtain makes it clear that this was no defensive line. Rather it provided a base for any military operation that might be necessary in enemy territory either on a large scale or via the front gates of the forts and milecastles.

Given so massive an undertaking as the construction of this vast frontier complex, it is all the more surprising that, as early as AD 139, preparations were in hand to abandon the greater part of Hadrian's Wall and to substitute for it a second curtain, some 130 km (80 miles) to the north. No one can be certain why this decision was made – whether there was serious trouble in the area or whether it reflected a desire for glory on the part of the man who became emperor upon Hadrian's death in July 138, Antoninus Pius. But what is clear is that, after campaigning by forces led by Q. Lollius Urbicus, building was under way by AD 142 or 143. Much less ambitious in scale than Hadrian's Wall, the Antonine frontier stretched 60 km (37 miles), from Old Kilpatrick to Bridgeness, across the Clyde-Forth isthmus – roughly speaking, between Glasgow and Edinburgh. It was constructed of turf blocks and clay, resting on a substantial footing of rubble, edged with stone kerbs. In front was a massive ditch, in places as much as 12 m (40 ft) across and 3.65 m (12 ft) deep. As on Hadrian's Wall, there seems also to have been a regular arrangement of turf-and-timber fortlets. Nine are now known, many of them quite recent discoveries; it seems that they were planned to lie about one Roman mile apart, interspersed amongst six forts. Only turrets have so far not been recognised and may never have been part of the design.

However, modifications to the blueprint also occurred on the Antonine Wall, most notably with the building of ten or more additional forts. In places these either obliterated or made redundant some of the

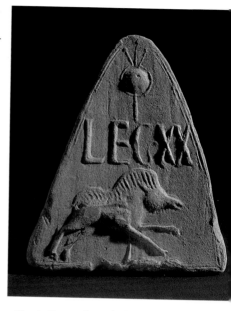

40 *A tile antefix, which ornamented the apex of a gable, from Holt, a site where pottery and tile were made for the legionary fortress at Chester. The boar was the symbol of the XXth legion, which was based at Chester. Height 21 cm (8.5 in).*

fortlets, clearly demonstrating a change of mind. These forts vary considerably in size and design although, typically for the period, they have multiple ditches to protect them and sometimes include an annexe. The main buildings like the headquarters block, granaries and commander's residence were usually in stone, but wood was considered adequate for the barracks and stores. Study of the accommodation suggests that the total garrison could well have numbered some six or seven thousand men, a force that could be readily deployed to west or east along a specially constructed military road.

In the absence of inscriptions to give us a precise date for the building of the Antonine frontier, the best guess is that the finishing touches took place about AD 148 or 149. What is still hotly debated is when it was abandoned. When the first edition of this book was written, in the early 1980s, the conventional view was that it was briefly evacuated in the mid-150s (perhaps because of an uprising in the Brigantian region of northern England), and then reoccupied until about AD 163 – although AD 180, 197, 207 or some point within that period remained possibilities. Now, such is the nature of scholarly argument, the latest idea is that the Antonine Wall was being decommissioned from about AD 158, and never again reinstated. In other words, in something like a century of modern study, there still remain fundamental gaps in our understanding of this question, a symbol of the ever-fascinating nature of Romano-British archaeology.

What is not in doubt is that Hadrian's Wall did again become the northern frontier of Britain, and remained so down to the last days of the province. Reconstructing its subsequent history is, however, complex. In AD 180 Commodus became emperor and it is from Dio Cassius that we learn that 'the greatest war of his reign was in Britain ... [when] the tribes in the island crossed the wall ... did a great deal of damage, and cut down a general and his troops, so Commodus in alarm sent against them Ulpius Marcellus who inflicted a major defeat upon the barbarians'. There was further trouble shortly afterwards, during a civil war that broke out in AD 193 and in which the governor of Britain, D. Clodius Albinus, was to play a considerable, if ultimately unsuccessful, role. When Albinus was defeated by L. Septimius Severus at Lyon in France in AD 197, it has been thought by some scholars that the northern tribes beyond the Wall seized the opportunity to attack a more or less undefended province. If so, the evidence is hardly decisive, and the view currently unfashionable. Nevertheless, there was a great deal of rebuilding in the frontier region about this time, and by AD 209, Severus and his two sons were in Britain, campaigning north of Hadrian's Wall. A legionary base on the south side of the River Tay at Carpow (near Perth), a fort at Cramond (near Edinburgh) and a series of marching camps stretching up the east side of Scotland, document the progress of the Roman army. When Severus died at York on 4 February 211, the bulk of the resistance had probably been broken. It was to usher in a period of almost a century, whose hallmark was to be peace and not war.

In a brief survey of a Roman province it is all too easy to concentrate on the architecturally imposing and the historically celebrated.

41 *Coins of (top) AD 155, with a defeated and bowed Britannia to commemorate a victory, possibly resulting from a rebellion of the Brigantes, and (below) AD 209, showing a bridge of boats constructed over the River Tay during the campaigns of Severus and his two sons, Caracalla and Geta, in Scotland.*

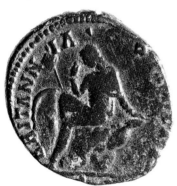

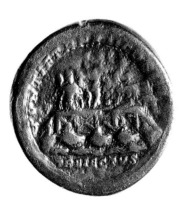

Yet, as we emphasised in an earlier chapter, the bulk of the population of Roman Britain was made up of people speaking Celtic and not Latin, and living much as they had done before the Romans arrived. Although as recent work is showing their settlements were not uncommon in the south of England, the sheer density and numbers of these sites in the northern part of the province make impressive statistics. Living close to the land, in buildings of little sophistication, these Britons used few 'Roman' objects – pottery, trinkets and the like – and can only have regarded their conquerors with suspicion, dislike and probably contempt. Hence the need for so large a garrison. Some moved to the small settlements (*vici*) that grew up around many of the forts; but most were content to remain in their farms and villages to eke out a poor but traditional life. The more mountainous areas of what was once French North Africa, where primitive villages still lie side by side with now abandoned French military posts, provide a vivid parallel. We may think of northern Britain under the Romans as a turbulent place, dominated by forts and frontiers; in reality, the most enduring feature was probably the long equilibrium that was struck up between a professional serving army and a large native population. It is a point once again brought out by the Vindolanda tablets; warfare hardly features, and most are about the mundane business of routine administration (especially accounts and applications for leave), building work and the organisation of supplies. There are some intriguing hints of financial wheeling and dealing, and even a complaint about the weather: 'I will provide some goods by means of which we may endure the storms'. It is all summed up by a letter from the commander's wife at Vindolanda, Claudia Severa, to another wife, Sulpicia Lepidina, whose husband is in charge of a nearby fort. Signed in her own hand, she says 'for the day of the celebration of my birthday, I give you a warm invitation to make sure that you come to us.' Nothing could so breathe life into our remote archaeology of Roman frontier life than this delightful epithet of history.

42 The letter found in the fort at Vindolanda inviting the commander's wife, Sulpicia Lepidina, to a birthday party, to be held by Claudia Severa, the wife of the commander of another fort. c. AD 97-102/3.

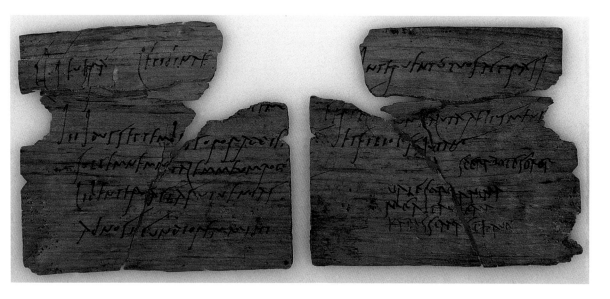

Chapter 8 | Art and architecture in Roman Britain

Classical traditions in art and architecture have so profoundly influenced styles of more recent times that they are familiar to us all: the elegant façade of the British Museum provides a ready example. It is important to remember, however, that in ancient Rome itself painting, sculpture and architecture strongly reflected Greek ideas and were often carried out by Greek craftsmen. What Rome did was to add to the genre, especially in personal portraiture, and to diffuse these ideas throughout the empire. It is particularly fascinating to see how they interacted with native cultures with a strong artistic tradition of their own, not least in Italy itself.

In the pre-Roman Celtic world of north-west Europe there existed a vigorous and distinctive style of art. Much of it comes down to us in the form of elaborate metalwork, particularly weapons, armour and regalia; but there must have been much more on materials such as wood and leather which have now perished in all but a few instances. Although influenced in its formative stages by the designs on Etruscan and Greek objects, Celtic art was essentially abstract. The most popular theme consisted of curvilinear patterns, often embellished with hatching and brightly coloured enamels. Representational sculpture, so favoured in

43 *Bronze statuette of an archer, found in Cheapside, London. His outstretched left hand would have originally held a bow, and his right hand the end of an arrow. This may be a representation of Hercules and is a superb example of purely classical art, of the second century.*

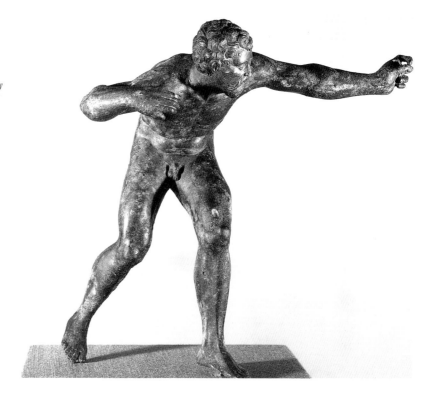

the classical world of Greece and Rome, was a largely foreign concept to the Celtic craftsman.

At first sight, we might think that this Celtic approach to art would have been swept away when the Romans imposed their new order upon northern Europe. But this would be far from the truth. Although the conquest certainly brought some Mediterranean artists and craftsmen (a distinction of little or no consequence in the ancient world) into a province such as Britain, most of those who worked in this field were of native origin. It was their task to adapt to the new styles, although one suspects that there must have been many who consciously strove to conserve what was familiar.

Classical models there were in plenty. Coins passed through the hands of anyone of any consequence and represented a major vehicle of political and artistic propaganda. Not only did they show the people of the empire what the reigning emperor looked like – often, perhaps, in a somewhat flattering way – but they were also an important source of information. The reverse side of a coin might describe a great victory, a feat of engineering or a contented world, prospering under the Roman peace. Rapidly circulated in army pay-packets, coins could bring people up-to-date about what was going on and how the Roman authorities wished to present the news. Similarly, statues of the emperor and his family served to underline their power and god-like qualities. Like coins, they set standards of taste and style for all to admire and emulate, and must have been a common sight in towns, shrines and military establishments. They also introduced new trends. Hadrian made it fashionable again to wear a beard, as so many ancient Greeks, whom he much admired, had done; both emperors and their wives brought in new hairstyles; and all of the upper ranks of provincial society followed the developments in dress of the imperial court.

It is probable that large numbers of stone and bronze sculptures, made by craftsmen trained in the Mediterranean, found their way to Britain. Moreover, statues of the imperial family, of gods and goddesses and of great statesmen provided a model for the local craftsmen. But the Celtic artist not educated in this way found the style far from his taste.

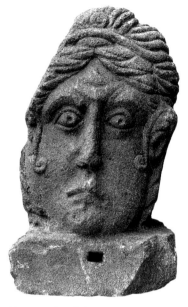

44 *Stone female head, probably from a funerary monument, from Towcester, Northamptonshire. The style is strongly Celtic, and it was probably made by a local craftsman. Height 57 cm (22.5 in).*

45 *Eight small bronze statuettes of gods and goddesses found in the early nineteenth century at Southbroom, Wiltshire. The style of the figures indicates a very strong Celtic element in their manufacture, although they evidently depict Roman deities. Third century AD.*

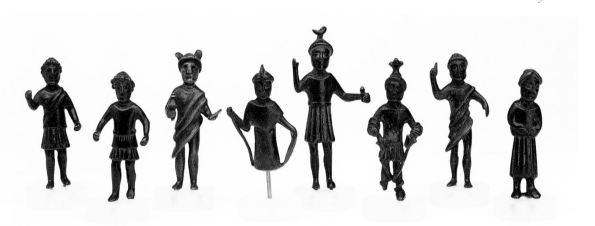

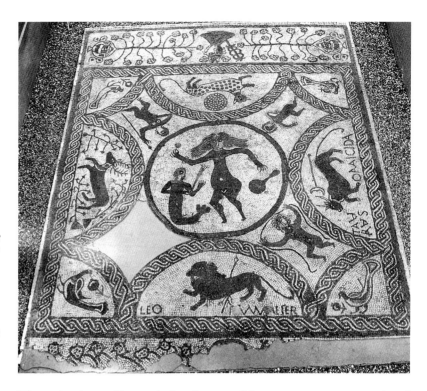

46 *A mosaic pavement found at Rudston villa in East Yorkshire. The arresting lady in the central roundel is identified by the mirror as a Celtic craftsman's version of Venus, while to the left is a Triton holding a conch or torch (although it looks more like a back-scratcher). It dates to the fourth century. (Hull Museum)*

The point is readily made by dozens of bronze statuettes, mostly of deities, that are known from Britain. They range from accomplished works in a purely classical idiom – some but not all imported – to extraordinary crudely drawn figures certainly of local origin. These express, however, not a lack of competence but a lack of interest in the realistic portrayal of the human form. Indeed, sometimes the result could be totally bizarre. This can be illustrated both by bronze and stone sculpture, and in other areas of art. A visit to Hull Museum, for example, where there is a fine collection of mosaic pavements, will give an opportunity to see a Celtic craftsman's version of the Roman goddess Venus, found at Rudston Roman villa, and a very remarkable creature she is too with her wild, unkempt hair, her glowering look, a fat belly and projecting rump! This work, just one of many examples where we see a fusion of Roman and Celtic traditions, well illustrates the growth of a local style of mosaic pavements. Several town-based 'schools' have been recognised although, as most mosaics in Britain date to the prosperous days of the fourth century, they appear only to emerge in the later Roman period. The quality is variable. Standardised layouts and repeated formal patterns occur again and again, and would have been part of the repertoire of any mosaicist, learned while a child-apprentice. The figured scenes display a greater individuality, some of them being quite sophisticated in design. Composed in a colourful way with cubes of brick and different stones, there are scenes taken from mythology (occasionally backed up with an erudite phrase from an ancient Latin writer) and, above all, scenes of religious inspiration – almost always, so far as one can judge, of classical origin. It was a way that aristocratic Britons could affirm their power and status as fully romanised leaders within the community, to their clients and vassals.

Mosaics on walls and vaults appear to have been very uncommon in Britain, although they occur frequently elsewhere in the empire. This may be because that aspect of mosaic art was becoming rarer in secular buildings in the late-Roman period; much of the effort was diverted at this time into decorating great churches, amongst which Santa Maria Maggiore in Rome and the basilicas of Ravenna still offer slightly later but particularly marvellous instances. Instead, the walls and ceilings of the private houses of the wealthy and of some public buildings were ornamented with the much less durable technique of painted plaster. These painted walls are rarely well preserved (the 'painted house' still visible at Dover is an exception), but careful reconstruction of the collapsed fragments shows that there was a wide range of decorative themes. Most surfaces were treated with repetitive geometric designs, but exotic materials like marble were sometimes imitated, and examples are known both of human figures and of landscapes. The Lullingstone Christian chapel is an especially precious instance of figured scenes, laboriously put together from thousands of pieces over a period of many years in a British Museum workshop.

These wall-paintings seem, as a whole, to reflect a more mainstream attitude to classical art than either mosaics or sculpture. The same is also true for a good many buildings, whether the great first-century palace at Fishbourne, the huge basilica of Roman London or the temple of Sul Minerva at Bath. Moreover, the classical tradition in architecture could extend to very mundane buildings. A simple barn, on a

47 A wall-painting from the fourth-century Christian chapel from the villa at Lullingstone, Kent. It shows figures with outstretched arms, the orantes *position of prayer. See also illustration 80. An interesting recent suggestion is that the villa may have become a monastery at this time, a not uncommon late-Roman phenomenon.*

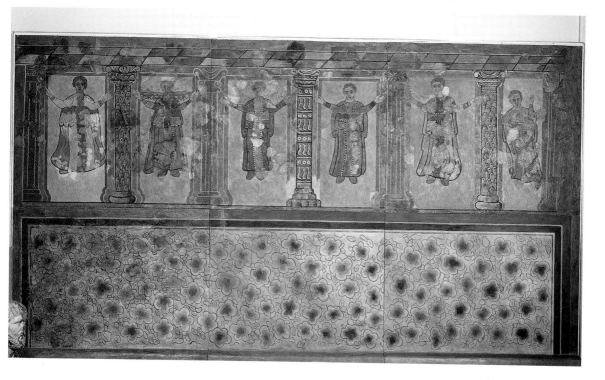

48 Right *A section of the façade of an early fourth-century barn-like building at Meonstoke, Hampshire, lifted in 1989. Although cut through by post-holes for a later structure of Anglo-Saxon date (fifth-sixth century), it is remarkable for its variety of colour and decorative detail.*

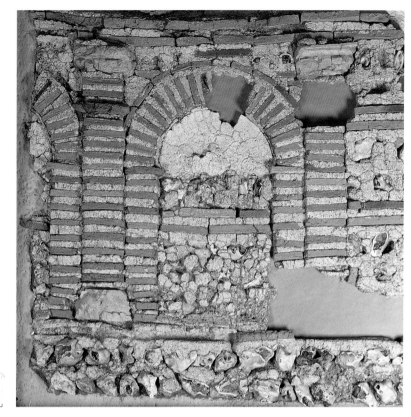

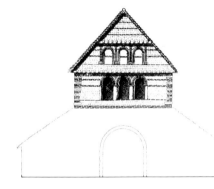

49 Above *A reconstruction of the early fourth-century Meonstoke building, based on excavated evidence. It foreshadows the design of early Romanesque churches in a very suggestive way.*

50 Right *A bronze figurine of a Romano-Celtic warrior god, dressed in Roman armour, and riding a dignified parade horse. It was found near Brough, Northamptonshire. Height of horse 9.3 cm (3.6 in).*

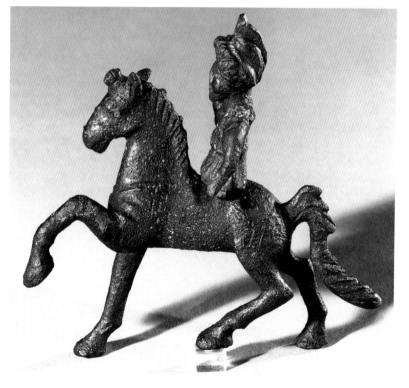

villa estate at Meonstoke (Hampshire), proved to have a façade of such ornateness as to be astonishing. Dating to the early fourth century, the building had a clerestory, so that it resembled a Romanesque church, and was embellished with Ionic capitals in greenstone; elaborate and colourful window embrasures; and a variety of rusticated patternings. How common such sophisticated design and craftsmanship may have been is wholly conjectural, given the dismal preservation of so many Romano-British structures; but we must be cautious in applying too provincial a label, simply because *Britannia* was so distant from the Mediterranean world.

Nevertheless, we can hardly doubt that most of the craftsmen who worked in Britain were trained in the north-west provinces of the empire. It is a fascinating exercise, given a collection of objects from Roman Britain, to search for the smooth command of the curvilinear design that so readily betrays the Celtic origins of the artist. Very often tucked away on some trivial item of metalwork, such as a brooch, they mark an adherence to the old traditions. In the centuries which followed Rome's withdrawal from Britain, these motifs were to be revived so that they became a standard part of Dark Age art. That the memory of Celtic, as opposed to classical art, was so strongly preserved during the centuries of Roman rule in Britain, is just one absorbing feature of the cultural history of this period. The governor Agricola may have thought that the Britons became 'enslaved' to Roman ways; in reality there was an extraordinary degree of compromise, something that will become particularly apparent when we look later at the subject of religion.

51 Below left *Two bone and two silver pins from London. The heads include Fortuna holding a cornucopia; Venus adjusting her sandal; a female head; and a hand holding a pomegranite. Maximum length 19.5 cm (7.6 in)*

52 Below *A very small bronze box, inlaid with superbly preserved enamel millefiori decoration, from a second-century grave at Elsenham, Essex. A rare type manufactured in the north-western provinces, it was probably used as an inkwell. Height 4.6 cm (1.8 in).*

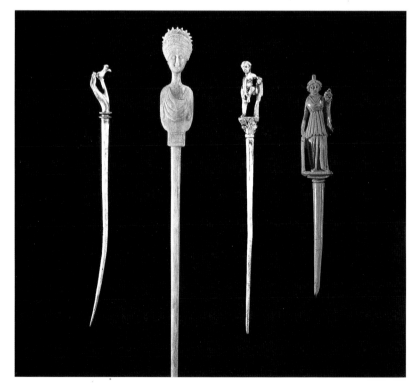

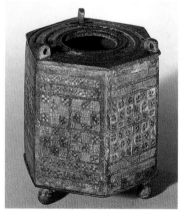

Chapter 9 | Industry, trade and crafts

Like all parts of the empire, the main basis of the Romano-British economy was unquestionably agriculture, particularly the cultivation of cereals and the raising of cattle, sheep and pigs. There was a large army to provision, as well as a substantial civilian population, and also evidence to show that a surplus was exported at times. Britain may not have been a vast grain-producer like Sicily or Egypt, nor a country where huge quantities of wine and oil were made, such as Spain, North Africa and Italy itself: but efficient management and a good network of communications helped to ensure that farming met with some considerable measure of success. Indeed, the most recent research suggests that, in the later Roman period – the apogee of the villa in Britain – there were significant innovations both in the range of crops and in agricultural technology; there is promised here a significant breakthrough in our understanding of the period.

There were also many other types of production, often on a large scale. As the excavator of many Roman sites will know, it was a world that was a conspicuous user of manufactured goods, fragments of which turn up in enormous quantities in archaeological deposits. Some items derive from very far afield, indicating the existence of well-organised long-distance trade routes; but the majority were made in local workshops, situated in the towns and larger, semi-urban, settlements, and catering for a limited regional market. Different provinces did develop their specialities: Britain was to become noted both for a type of duffle coat and for woollen rugs, while Diocletian's Edict of AD 301 priced British beer at double the cost of that produced in Egypt. The Vindolanda tablets show that it was much drunk by the soldiers there in the early second century AD, and there was a resident *cervesarius*, or brewer, named Atrectus: he was a maker of 'Celtic beer', and the word

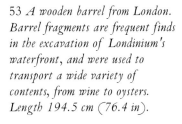

53 *A wooden barrel from London. Barrel fragments are frequent finds in the excavation of Londinium's waterfront, and were used to transport a wide variety of contents, from wine to oysters. Length 194.5 cm (76.4 in).*

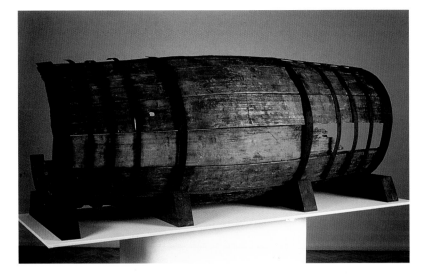

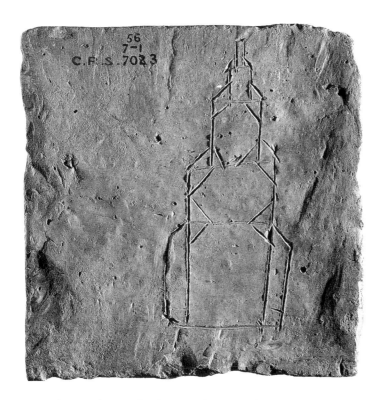

54 *A floor tile probably from London; it was inscribed before it was fired with the drawing of a building best identified as a lighthouse. Lighthouses were frequently constructed in the ancient world to aid navigation; one still stands at Dover. 20 x 20.5 cm (7.8 x 8 in).*

remains with us today, in the form of the Spanish '*cerveza*'. But we must be careful not to assume too sophisticated an economic system. Unlike today, where theoretical considerations are of paramount importance, there was no 'economic strategy' that governed the Roman empire. While one sort of production might be encouraged in a particular province, all were expected to be profitable. Otherwise, commerce was allowed to develop more or less in a natural way.

One area that the Roman authorities did control closely was the mining of metals. As had been known from long before the conquest, Britain possessed deposits of gold, silver (mainly extracted from lead ores), copper, tin and iron. Indeed, it is clear from bars of lead bearing inscriptions that lead and silver were being extracted from the Mendips of south-west England by AD 49, only six years after the beginning of the conquest. Lead was also mined in Wales and in northern England, where, as a dated bar shows, work had started within a year of the acquisition of that territory. Only one gold-mine is known, at Dolaucothi in south-

55 *A lead ingot (or 'pig') from Tansley Moor, near Matlock Bridge, Derbyshire. It is stamped '(Product) of P(ublius) Rubrius Abascantus from the Lutudarensian mine'. The company, Socii Lutudarenses, leased the mining rights from the state in this area. Weight 78 kg (172 lb).*

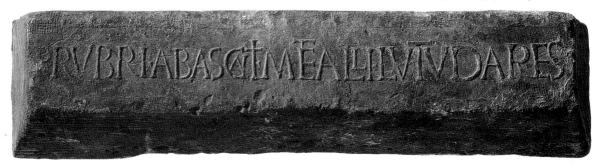

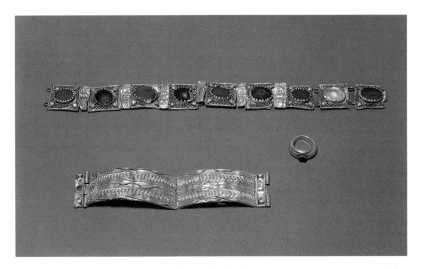

56 *Gold bracelets from Rhayader in central Wales. Elaborately decorated, including carnelian and paste settings, and filigree work, they illustrate the fine quality of jewellery available to the richer classes of Roman Britain. First-second century* AD.

west Wales, where there is evidence both for open-cast extraction and for underground galleries. Nearby there was a fort, underlining the fact that gold and silver mining were kept under tight military supervision, although the administration will have been in the hands of a procurator (and later in the history of the province may have been leased out).

Gold and silver were of course used for the high-value coinage, while in the late-Roman period official payments were sometimes made in the form of specially shaped ingots. A number of these have been found in Britain. Both metals were also fashioned into jewellery and there is some very fine silver plate. Certain pieces of the gold jewellery may well have been imported, but it is possible that some was made near Dolaucothi itself. Gold was being refined in London in the late first century AD, probably under official control, and the workshops of gold-smiths have been found in towns like Verulamium and Cirencester. Some types of silver bracelets and brooches were also made within the province, as a jeweller's hoard of the mid-second century, found at

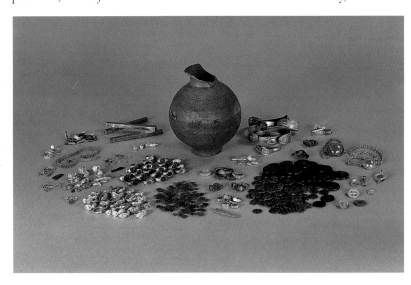

57 *A Romano-British jeweller's hoard, placed in a pot, from Snettisham, Norfolk. Buried c.* AD *155, it includes rings, bracelets, unmounted gems, ingots, and coins for melting down. There is also a burnishing tool. Height of pot 17.5 cm (6.9 in).*

Snettisham (Norfolk), shows; traces of gold on a polishing tool indicate that he also produced objects in that metal as well. But much of the fine plate, like the Mildenhall Treasure, was undoubtedly produced in other parts of the empire. Some centres of manufacture have been identified and they are invariably the great cities of the ancient world like Carthage, Constantinople, Antioch and Rome itself. It is probably significant that there is evidence of imperial coin-mints in all these cities. What is surprising is to see how much exquisite silverware, particularly of late-Roman date, has been discovered in so peripheral a province as Britain. One very important find is the group of silver vessels from Water Newton, near Peterborough. They are exceptional partly because of their Christian associations – being the oldest known communion silver in the world – but also because of their plain style and matt finish. These are features unparalleled elsewhere in the Roman empire, and very probably point to an origin in Britain.

Most metal tableware was not produced in precious metals, however, but in alloys of copper, tin and zinc, which produce a hard bronze or brass. Both copper and tin extraction appear to have been state controlled (although largely through lessees), but manufacturing workshops were widespread. The craftsmen in the towns were capable of making very passable imitations of classical forms of cups, jugs and skillets as well as a wide range of fittings and ornaments (particularly brooches which were essential for anchoring the draped style of Roman dress) and religious statuettes.

Among other decorative techniques, widespread use was made of bright-coloured enamels, a tradition that was already well-developed in pre-Roman Britain. We also know of rural bronzesmiths, many of whom no doubt moved from settlement to settlement, dealing with specific orders. Others set up stalls in roadstations, selling trinkets like a 'cosmetic set' where eyebrow tweezers, nail-cleaners and a scoop for freeing the ear of wax was a popular item. Similarly, there were both town and country blacksmiths. The iron itself derived from a number of areas, of which the Weald of Kent and Sussex and the Forest of Dean of Gloucestershire seem to have been the most important: part of it may have been supervised by the British fleet, whose headquarters lay at Dover. Smelted and partly refined at the mines, the iron was then transported in bars, to be forged at its destination. A cheap and durable product, it was made into an enormously diverse range of objects and fittings by the smith, who could no doubt turn his hand to most things. But there were also specialists, such as armourers, locksmiths and cutlers, who occasionally stamped their name or trademark upon their products.

To these metalworkers, we must add one other group who achieved some importance in the later Roman period, those who made vessels of pewter. Based mainly in the south-west of England, where both the lead and the tin that constitute this alloy were readily available, the craftsmen produced tableware that, when polished, must have been a cheap and acceptable substitute for silver. It was largely a British industry, made essentially for home consumption, and was just one of a number of ventures that achieved considerable success. Amongst others we might

58 *A hoard of jewellery and coins, placed in a silver skillet, from Backworth (Tyne and Wear). The vessel has a dedication to the Matres (mother goddesses), made by Fabius Dubitatus; a gold ring is also dedicated to the same deities. Second century AD.*

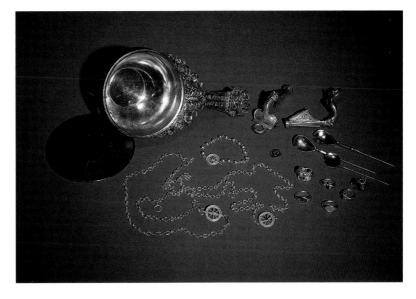

cite two whose roots lay firmly in pre-Roman times. One was the production of objects made of jet, a material found mainly in the area of Whitby in north-east England. These attractive hair-pins, necklaces, bangles and medallions were widely circulated in Britain and some found their way abroad, especially to the Rhineland. Similarly the shale deposits of the Kimmeridge region of Dorset which could be lathe-turned like wood were extensively quarried for manufacture into furniture, trays, vessels and personal finery.

Other industries have left less archaeological evidence. Leather, for example, is not commonly preserved except under wet conditions, but was nevertheless used for a wide variety of purposes. Of the many leather objects found at the military site of Vindolanda, near Hadrian's Wall, some seventy per cent had the professional touch of the craftsman,

59 *A pewter cup from Icklingham, Suffolk. Objects in pewter (an alloy of tin and lead) were widely manufactured in Britain, especially in the late-Roman period, and would have had an attractive silver-coloured appearance. Height 8.5 cm (3.3 in).*

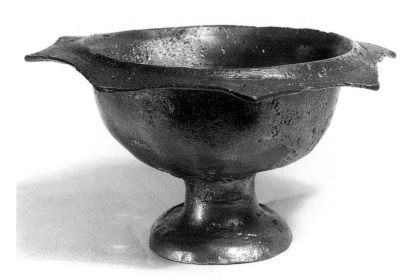

while the rest would seem to have been home-made. Three shoes bore the maker's stamp and must have come from high-class establishments. Objects in bone, a cheap and handy material, survive much better, but woodwork has mostly disappeared. Its importance may be measured by the fact that Pliny tells us of the astronomical prices that were paid for top-quality furniture, while we also know of specialist guilds of wagon-makers and shipwrights. Together with rugs and other textiles – again highly perishable materials – objects in wood must have been very common in the home. Although the metal fittings from furniture and the like, as well as carpenter's tools, have often come down to us, we must recognise that our picture of ancient crafts is highly biased towards the more durable remains. Of these, it is pottery that, the buildings apart, survives in greatest quantity. Employed both as tableware and in the kitchen, pottery was cheap to make and easily replaced when broken: rubbish pits are normally full of shattered vessels. It is also very useful to the archaeologist since production centres can be identified from the kilns and 'wasters' – badly misfired vessels – enabling us to trace the

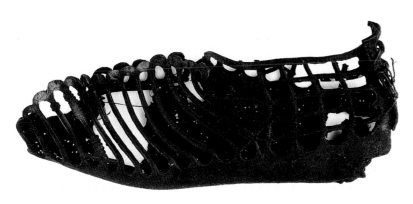

60 *A leather shoe found in London. Elegant footwear was commonplace amongst the aristocracy. Wet conditions have preserved such objects.*

marketing patterns; and also because changes in the form of the pots permit us to date some individual types quite closely.

The organisation of the pottery industry (and more than one thousand kiln sites are now known) has much to tell us about commerce in the ancient world. On the one hand were craftsmen who turned out coarse, hand-made vessels for their local customers; on the other were highly organised industries, marketing mass-produced items for a wide distribution. Careful study has shown, for example, that the army on Hadrian's Wall had a contract with potters in Dorset to supply cheap, black-ware cooking pots polished with a high sheen. More attractive, perhaps, were vessels in a glossy bright red ware made in France and the Rhineland and known today as 'samian ware'. These were products of factories whose owners often stamped their samian ware with their name, and there was a wide range both of plain forms and decorated types. Modelled in low relief, the decoration was carried out by means of fired-clay moulds, so as to facilitate rapid production. As a result it is not difficult to recognise the favoured pictorial themes of many of the samian potters.

61 *A mould-made decorated samian ware bowl, manufactured at La Graufesenque in south Gaul. Datable to c. AD 50-70, it is stamped on the interior by the potter Licinus. Diameter 22.2 cm (8.7 in).*

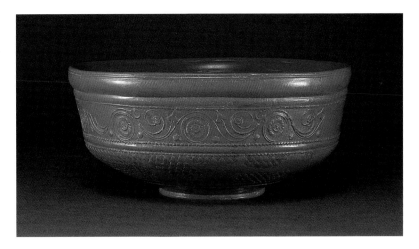

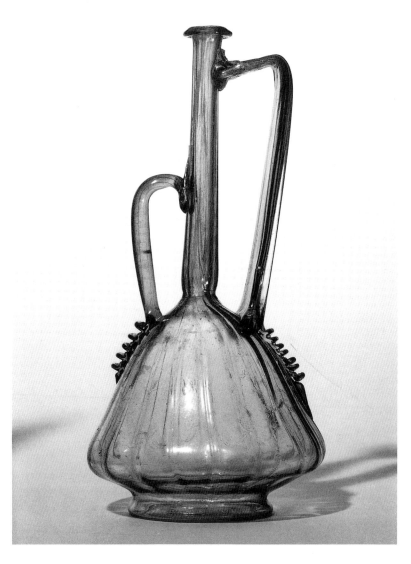

62 *A glass flagon from a grave at Bayford, Kent. Second century. Height 23 cm (9 in).*

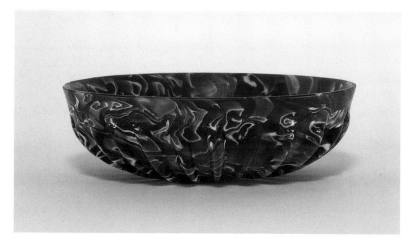

63 *A pillar-moulded (ribbed) glass bowl, in dark blue and white marbled glass, from Radnage, Buckinghamshire. It was found in a grave of the first century AD. Height 4.8 cm (1.8 in), diameter 16.8 cm (6.6 in)*

Samian ware was sold in vast quantities in Britain until the industry went into decline towards AD 200-50. Why this is so is not clear; but British manufacturers, already competitive in this prosperous market, soon filled the gap. Most conspicuously successful were those who exploited the clay deposits of the Nene Valley in the Peterborough region. Their rich houses indicate a high level of profit, and their craftsmen produced a fine range of vessels, some of them decorated with superbly rendered scenes of the hunt. Here was the Celtic craftsman portraying what was familiar and natural, allowing him to use his innate sensibility for the curvilinear line. But many other pottery-producing centres also developed, reflecting the fact that it was easier and cheaper to sell within an area where transport costs were low and there was a ready market.

Good-quality glass – a not uncommon find in burials in Britain – was likewise imported from manufacturing centres on the Continent. At towns like Cologne in Germany, the glass-makers became particularly proficient at using the recently developed technique of glass-blowing. The result was an appealing range of jugs, flagons, bowls and cups. There were also more robust bottles, made by blowing the molten glass into a mould, which may have been designed mainly as containers for perishable goods. Some were certainly manufactured in Britain, as a huge dump of glass fragments for recycling into new vessels, as well as a furnace, recently discovered near London Bridge, clearly show. But glass-making tends to leave little trace since the glass was generally reused, and it is therefore hard to gauge the true scale of the industry. In sum, however, we can put forward a picture of a very broad-based economy in Roman Britain. While the quality of the workmanship may not always have approached that of the best workshops in other provinces, the craftsmen nevertheless filled the need for most requirements and their products reached a wide cross section of society. This is surely a significant comment on the way life in Britain was transformed under Roman rule.

Chapter 10 | Roman and Celtic religious cults

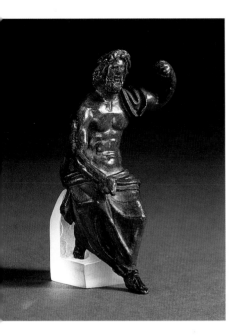

Greek and Roman religion involved a very large number of gods and goddesses. As long as the worshipper observed the correct ritual, these divinities could be expected to play an important role in regulating human affairs. Some were major deities, venerated in much the same form throughout the Graeco-Roman world. Others were minor spirits, whose influence was purely local; here the main preoccupations were with fertility and the cycle of growth, death and rebirth. But the natives of the provinces, such as the various peoples of Britain, also had their pantheon of gods and goddesses. To these deities the Romans took a tolerant attitude. As long as they posed no political threat, as the Druids seemed to do, they were content to accept them, often recognising that they shared characteristics with some of their own gods. The result was something of an amalgam of classical and native divinities, where both the names and the attributes were absorbed without incongruity into a single deity. Overall, it was a potent force for unity in an empire made up of many diverse races and creeds.

Yet it is important to emphasise that Roman official religion involved little emotional commitment and was never seen as a way towards spiritual growth: that was a matter which lay within the realm

64 *A bronze figure of Jupiter from West Stoke, Sussex. He is shown seated, wearing a toga and with a wreath or diadem in his hair; the left hand will have held a sceptre. Height 8.25 cm (3.25 in).*

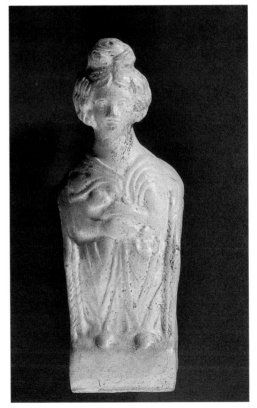

65 *Pipeclay figurine of a mother-goddess, nursing an infant, found at Welwyn, Hertfordshire. Such statuettes were made in large quantities in Gaul, and imported into Britain. Second century AD. Height 14.7 cm (5.7 in).*

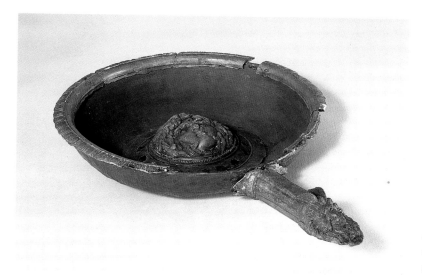

66 *A bronze skillet from Faversham, Kent. The terminal of the handle has a fine bearded head of Pan, while the motif in the centre of the bowl is of Medusa, encircled by a vine scroll inlaid in silver and niello.*

of philosophical study. The approach to religion was essentially practical so that, by performing the right actions, a more secure and comfortable existence might be achieved. Only with the rise of what might be termed the personal cults, of which Christianity was to become by far the most influential, did the traditional view of religion become at first undermined and then overturned.

Roman Britain is an absorbing area in which to study these processes since the range of evidence is extensive and varied. It is appropriate to begin with the cult of the emperor himself since, of all the religions of the Roman world, this was the most overtly political. Just as the father of a family was also its priest and thus responsible for the carrying out of the religious rites that concerned a household, so the emperor was the chief priest of the state. But, ever since the first Roman emperor, Augustus, it had also become customary to elevate him to the status of a god, and to pay him due religious devotion. Strictly speaking, this did not happen until after the emperor's death; but in practice the Imperial cult often became well established during his lifetime. This is why in the early days of the conquest of Britain, a great temple was erected to the emperor Claudius at Colchester (although there is debate about whether this happened before or after his death). Sacked by Boudicca's warriors in the revolt of AD 60-61, it was intended not only as a centre for the state religion but also as a symbol of Roman domination. Well-organised corporations were set up to promote the worship of the emperor. Known as the *seviri augustales*, they were made up largely of affluent freedmen, who were expected to provide funds from their own pockets for the festivals and monuments. They will often have paid for the large number of imperial dedications, statues and statuettes that are known from Britain. Several come from the Fenland, which, as we have already seen, may have been imperial land where the emperor would undoubtedly have been venerated.

During the period of the early empire, the Imperial cult gained increasing precedence over the traditional Roman pantheon. However,

67 *Bronze statuette of Mars from Fossdyke, Torksey, Lincolnshire. The inscription on the base records that the statue was dedicated to the deity by the Colasuni, Bruccius and Caratius, and was made by the coppersmith Celatus, who also contributed a pound of bronze, at a cost of three denarii. Height 27 cm (10.5 in).*

68 Below *A silver votive plaque from Barkway, Hertfordshire. It is dedicated to the god Mars Alator, a Romano-Celtic combination. Height 18 cm (5 in).*

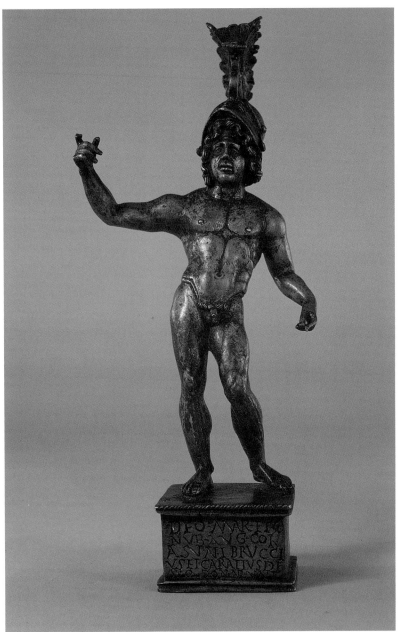

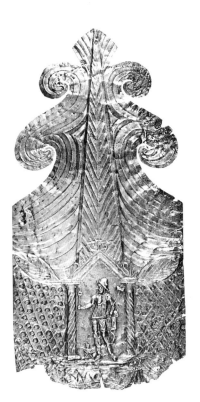

the principal deities of the city of Rome, Jupiter, Juno and Minerva (whose main temple lay on the Capitoline Hill in Rome: hence its name, the Capitolium), were still accorded considerable status. This is particularly true in the high-ranking towns, the coloniae and municipia, where there will have been a joint temple to the three, a capitolium, and also in the military areas. Indeed, it was the custom at each fort to dedicate a new altar to Jupiter – optimus, maximus, the best and greatest – beside the parade ground on New Year's Day. A cache of these altars has been found at the auxiliary fort of Maryport in Cumbria. One example reads:

'To Jupiter, best and greatest, the first Cohort of Spaniards, which is commanded by Gaius Caballius Priscus, tribune, [set this up].' No capitolium has yet been identified with certainty in Britain, but there are sufficient representations of, and dedications to, Jupiter and Minerva to show that these two deities in particular were widely worshipped. They can be readily identified by their attributes: Jupiter is depicted as a powerful bearded man, normally provided with a thunderbolt and an eagle, while Minerva can be recognised by her armour and an owl. Mars and Mercury were also popular gods, mainly because they had their close Celtic equivalents. Mars was a warrior figure, often shown resplendent in full war trappings; Mercury, on the other hand, was a god of trade and commerce (symbolised by his purse) and also, as winged feet and a hat imply, of travel. He usually carried a herald's winged staff, entwined with snakes. An exceptional find of the head from a superb limestone statue of Mercury, as well as many small statuettes, comes from a temple built on traditional Celtic lines, at Uley in Gloucestershire. Sheep, goats and cockerels – all animals sacred to Mercury – were sacrificed at the sanctuary, a site where the origins go back to before the Roman conquest and where the worship of Mercury persisted well after the time that the empire was encouraged to become Christian in ad 312.

Many other classical deities are represented by finds from Britain, especially those of the goddess of love, Venus; but the Celtic plan of Mercury's sanctuary at Uley reminds us of the way that the Celts assimilated Roman divinities into their religious beliefs – and vice versa. Just as Aelius Vibius, centurion of the XXth legion, and Tineius Longus, a cavalry commander of senatorial rank, found it prudent to propitiate the British god, Antenociticus, at the Hadrian's Wall fort of Benwell, so Celtic and Roman deities were often combined. Thus at Bath there was a great sanctuary, laid out on Mediterranean lines, and dedicated to Minerva together with the local water-spirit, Sul. A typical inscription

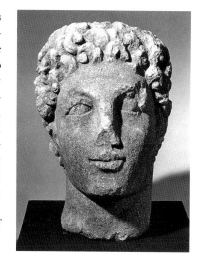

69 *The head of the over-life-size cult statue of the god Mercury from the Romano-Celtic temple at Uley, Gloucestershire. Though of provincial work, and carved in British limestone, this statue is based on Greek and Hellenistic prototypes. Second century AD.*

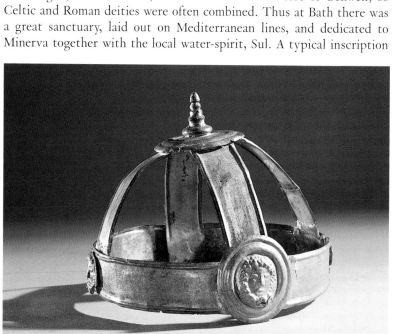

70 *A bronze crown from Hockwold-cum-Wilton, Norfolk. Found together with five diadems, they probably form part of the ceremonial regalia used by Romano-British priests. Height 15.9 cm (6.25 in).*

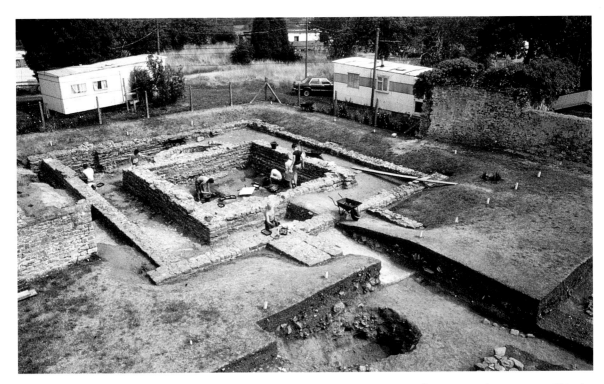

71 *Excavation in progress upon the Romano-Celtic temple at Venta Silurum (Caerwent, Gwent). It was constructed about AD 330, nearly two decades after Christianity was adopted as the official religion of the Roman empire.*

reads: 'To the goddess Sulis Minerva, Sulinus, son of Maturus, willingly and deservedly fulfilled his vow' – presumably by making a valuable offering, thousands of which (mainly coins) have been found in excavations at the sanctuary. There are many other examples of the conflation of two divinities. From Barkway in Hertfordshire come silver plaques with dedications to Mars Alator and Mars Toutatis – all warrior figures – while spoons in the Thetford Treasure associate the central-Italian god of the woods and fields, Faunus, with Celtic spirits such as Medugenus and Blotugus. Similarly, the Celtic Taranis, symbolised by a wheel, was linked with Jupiter since both had power over lightning and thunder:

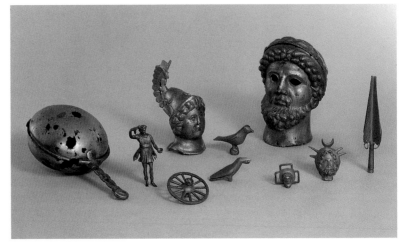

72 *A hoard of votive bronzes from Felmingham Hall, Norfolk. They include heads of Jupiter and Minerva; a mask of Sol with sun rays; a lar or household god; a wheel associated with the Celtic god, Taranis; and a rattle.*

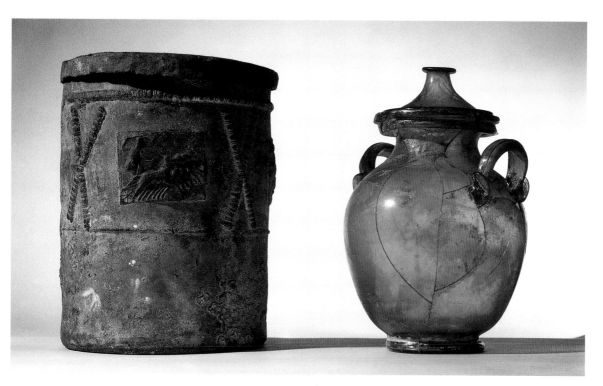

taran in modern Welsh still means a clap of thunder, while wheels occur repeatedly as motifs in art and jewellery, as a sign of good luck. Taranis was clearly a very potent god!

    Some other Celtic divinities, like the mother-goddesses (a basic fertility cult) or the horse-goddess, Epona, retained both their popularity and an independence of name. Indeed, they were widely adopted by many Roman soldiers and others. What Rome did was to preserve and propitiate these native gods and goddesses, and to influence the Celtic world into making three-dimensional representations of their deities. This explains why we have so rich a legacy of religious objects. Over 150 probable temple sites are known to us from Roman Britain, a figure which is likely to be a fraction of the total. Although most are located in the 'civilian' area of southern Britain, where local aristocrats could provide patronage, they nevertheless underline just how pervasive an influence religion was whether to Celt or to Roman.

73 The glass cinerary urn and its lead container, from a burial at Warwick Square, London. The container is decorated with a figure of the god Sol, riding in his chariot. Height of lead container 39 cm (13.75 in).

Chapter 11 | The personal religions

74 *A small marble statuette of Bacchus, with a cup, vine and his usual animal companion, a panther. Although found at a Roman villa at Spoonley Wood, Gloucestershire, this piece is of continental manufacture; it was found in a burial, perhaps of the villa's owner. Probably third century. Height 39.9 cm (15.7 in).*

Apuleius' *Metamorphoses* is a rather bawdy but delightful novel, written in the second century AD, which tells of the adventures of one Lucius. He has the misfortune to be accidentally turned into an ass, and is only restored to human form through the intervention of the Egyptian goddess, Isis. The book culminates in a description of Lucius' initiation into the mysteries of the cult, something that may well be autobiographical. The worship of Isis was just one of a number of religions which entered the Roman world from further east. Many had complex rites of initiation and enshrined the concept that an individual human being had unique significance and could hope for personal salvation in the afterlife. Usually known as the mystery cults, they provide a sharp contrast with the altogether more formalised and impersonal religions of the Roman state.

The very private nature of so many of these cults means that we possess all too few details about them. But it is clear that they were very pervasive in the western part of the Roman empire and one, Christianity, was eventually to become the official religion of the Roman state. Amongst the older of these cults was that of the god of wine, Bacchus. In origin from

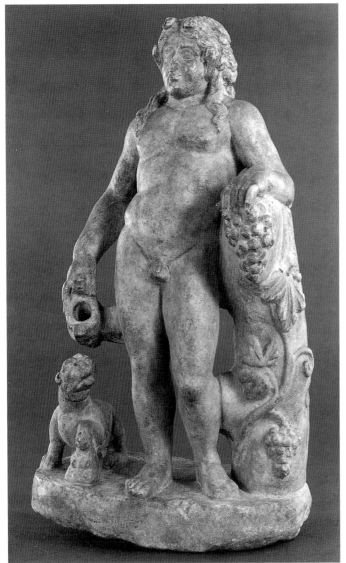

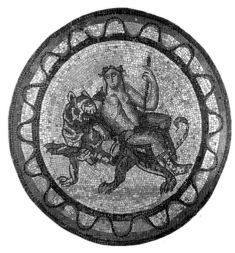

75 *Central roundel of a mosaic pavement from Leadenhall Street, London, depicting Bacchus riding a tiger. First-second century AD. Diameter 1.12 m (43.5 in).*

Greece, where Bacchus was also known as Dionysos, his worship involved feasting and drinking, music and dancing. Something of the state of ecstasy brought about by these revels is shown by the scenes on the great dish of the Mildenhall Treasure. Dating to about the middle of the fourth century AD, this priceless collection of silver tableware illustrates how Bacchic themes retained their popularity even in a Christian world which strongly censured such licentious goings-on. Similarly, another mystical Greek god, Orpheus, was also a widely admired divinity in fourth-century Britain. There are some particularly fine mosaics, showing him playing his lyre to a charmed audience of animals, with whose protection he was especially concerned. The best of these in Britain, at Woodchester in Gloucestershire, is now permanently buried, but it is well worth a journey to Brading Roman villa, on the Isle of Wight, where there are pavements with Orpheus, a Bacchic-like head and some fascinating scenes which may portray mysterious rites of initiation.

Naturally, there is much in these Greek cults which touches on the age-old theme of fertility. This constant preoccupation of human beings is further reflected in other mystery cults, like that of Cybele and her consort, Attis, both divinities that derived from the eastern

76 *The Corbridge Lanx; a superb example of silver tableware of the fourth century AD, found in 1735 at Corbridge, Northumberland. The scene is a pagan one, with the god Apollo, his sister Diana and mother Leto, and Minerva. It may commemorate the visit the pagan emperor Julian made in AD 363 to the shrine of Apollo on the Greek island of Delos. Length 44 cm (19 in).*

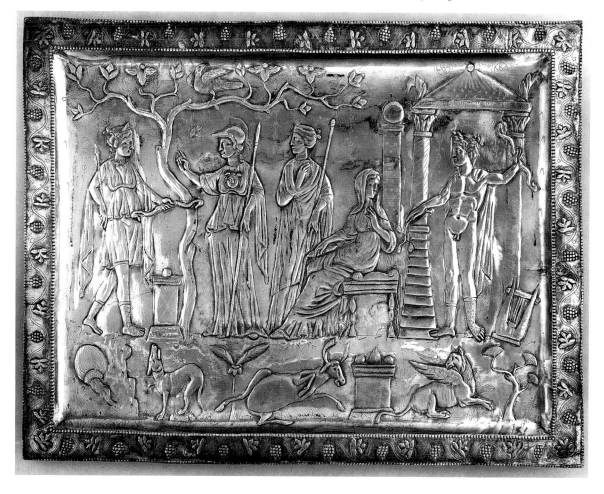

77 *Silver statuette of the Egyptian god Harpocrates (Horus), with a gold ring for suspension. He is shown with the attributes of other gods, making him a universal and pantheistic deity, like his mother Isis, who was also worshipped throughout the empire. Height 6.5 cm (2.5 in).*

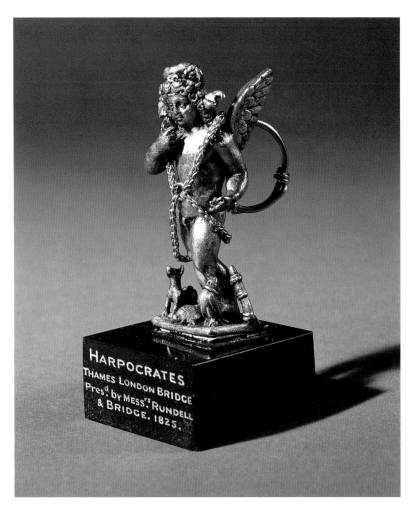

Mediterranean. Cybele's major role was as a mother goddess, although she also protected towns, while Attis was the subsidiary deity. Their priests had to suffer ritual castration, and there are those who believe that a bronze clamp, found in the River Thames near London Bridge, was used for such a task.

Certainly, London, for much of the Roman period a thriving port, capital and centre of trade and commerce, was the focus of many diverse religions. The great cathedrals and churches and the back-street chapels and meeting-houses of contemporary London had their counterpart in the Roman city. Temples for the official deities may have stood almost side by side with those of the 'secret' cults, like that of Isis, whose existence is recorded on a rough message scratched onto a pottery vessel: *'Londini ad fanum Isidis'*, 'London, at the temple of Isis'. The whereabouts of this temple is not known, but in 1954 both Londoners and visitors had the chance to witness the excavation of the temple of another mystery god, that of Mithras, a cult of Indo-Iranian origin.

Still visible today in front of Mansion House, Queen Victoria Street, where it has been reconstructed a short distance from its original site, the temple consists of a rectangular nave, divided into three aisles, with an apse at one end. Small in size, it was designed for an exclusive and élitist congregation. Moreover, it was set into low-lying ground so that there was little natural light. This is explained by the fact that, according to Persian legend, Mithras released the forces of life by slaying a huge bull, hidden away in a cave. He thus represented both light and life, symbolised by his constant companions, Cautes (who holds a torch aloft and is therefore Day) and Cautopates (whose downthrust torch indicates Night).

Mithraism was a demanding religion, open only to men, and involved seven grades of initiation. Some of these rites took the form of physical torment, one reason perhaps why the cult was popular amongst soldiers in the military areas of Roman Britain. Unlike in the normal ancient temple, where the altar lay in front of the façade, initiates were permitted to enter the building and to participate in the ritual; but this did not mean that all other religions were closed to them. Although they were expected to live a life of great moral rectitude, their faith, in keeping with the broad Roman attitude of tolerance, could embrace other deities. Thus, the London Mithraeum yielded not only representations of Mithras and his attendants, but also those of Minerva, the Egyptian god Serapis, Mercury and a group depicting an inebriated Bacchus with figures of Pan, a satyr, a nymph, a panther and Silenus riding on a donkey. 'Life to the wandering men' reads the inscription beneath the Bacchic group, now a prize exhibit of the Museum of London.

Mithraism incensed many Christians. They could sneer at the simplicities and contradictions of many of the old pagan cults, but Mithraism seemed to them to be a deliberate and devilish parody of their own beliefs. The birth-date of Mithras was on Christmas Day, 25 December; the central ritual of his worship was a shared meal; and the standards demanded of his followers were not unlike those required of Christians. Despite the exclusive nature of Mithraism, it appeared to constitute a far greater threat to Christianity than did either the traditional classical cults or the other 'mystery' religions. This is why so many followers of Mithraism hid away the cult statues of their divinities when the emperor Constantine issued his 'Edict of Toleration' towards Christians in AD 312, and those who still held to their pagan beliefs became increasingly subject to intolerance and persecution.

Constantine's decision to uphold Christianity as the only faith was not of course wholly altruistic. Christian beliefs had been gaining ground for some time, encouraged by the fact that this was a religion open to all, men and women, master and servant. United by their faith in one god and one god only, Christians had begun to constitute a group with considerable political power. Just how numerous such a group may have been in a province like Britain is, however, not easy to determine. This is particularly the case in the days before Constantine's proclamation, when Christians, fearing persecution, took great pains to disguise their religious affiliation. Services were held in private houses, and the ecclesiastical objects that they used were almost always capable of some other more innocent interpretation. But literary evidence suggests that there

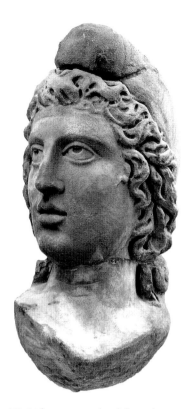

78 *Life-size stone head from the Walbrook Mithraeum, London, of the god Mithras. He wears a cap and gazes upwards towards the sun while slaying the primeval bull. (Museum of London)*

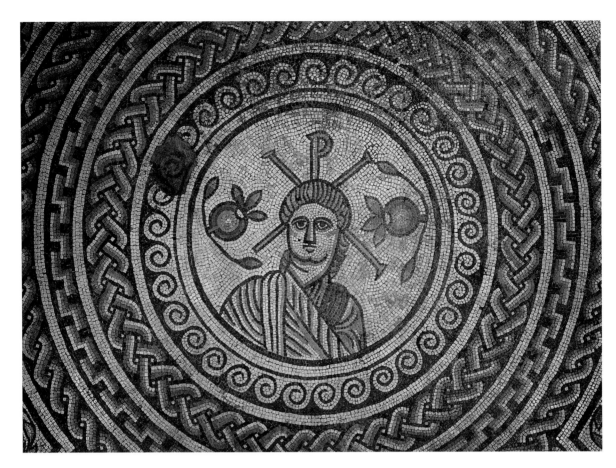

79 *The central motif of the mosaic pavement from the villa at Hinton St Mary, Dorset. The portrait with the Chi-Rho symbol, the first two letters of Christ's name in Greek, behind the head is almost certainly that of Christ. Fourth century* AD.

80 *A Chi-Rho on a wall painting from the fourth-century Christian chapel at Lullingstone, Kent. It is set in a wreath, together with an alpha and omega, two doves and garlands, and is flanked by columns. See also illustration 47.*

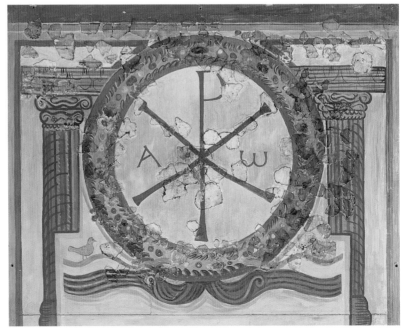

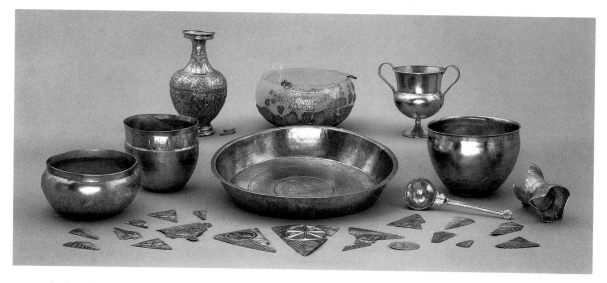

was a fairly substantial Christian community, something confirmed by the fact that there were bishops from London, York and probably Lincoln or Colchester available to attend a council of the Church at Arles in southern France in AD 314. Indeed, evidence for fourth-century churches in some of these centres, and in rural contexts, is increasingly coming to light; these include an extra mural cemetery chapel at Butt Road, Colchester, and what may prove to be a massive cathedral at London. There have also been other remarkable discoveries, such as the Christian chapel from the villa at Lullingstone (Kent), with its famous wall-paintings; the Hinton St Mary mosaic, with its head of Christ (quite possibly the oldest in the world); and the silver communion service from the town of Durobrivae near Peterborough. Most recently has been the celebrated unearthing of the Hoxne Treasure, found in 1992; this astonishing collection of gold and silver objects, as well as some 15000 coins, was manifestly owned c. AD 400 by a Christian aristocrat, as Chi-Rho symbols (the first two letters of Christ's name in Greek), monogram crosses and a phrase on a spoon, *vivas in deo* ('may you live in God'), clearly show. Nevertheless, finds like the Thetford Treasure, datable to about AD 390 and with its overt references to the god Faunus, remind us that paganism was

81 *The hoard of silver vessels and plaques found in 1975 at the Roman town of Durobrivae (Water Newton, near Peterborough). Firmly identified as Christian by numerous Chi-Rho symbols and by longer inscriptions, this treasure is the oldest set of church plate known from the Roman world. Fourth century AD.*

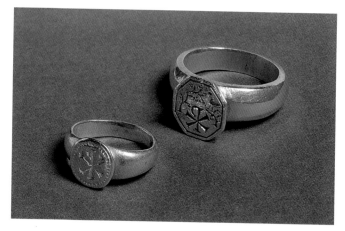

still a considerable force nearly three generations after Constantine had embraced Christianity. Likewise, many pagan temples flourished during the fourth century. Whatever the emperor decreed, it seems most probable that in late-Roman Britain there was a complex blend of beliefs and practices, some Roman, some native and some of eastern origin.

82 *Two Christian gold rings with the Chi-Rho symbol, from Brentwood, Essex (left) and Suffolk. The latter also has a bird pecking at fruit on a branch, a common pagan motif which was adopted in Christian iconography.*

Chapter 12 | The end of Roman Britain

The first half of the fourth century was a prosperous period for many Romano-Britons. Wealthy villas, with fine mosaics and wall-paintings, flourished in large parts of the southern part of the province (over a thousand are now known), and this was certainly their heyday. A mansion like that at Woodchester (Gloucestershire) had more than sixty-five rooms, and such opulence – the architectural counterpart of great late-Roman treasures like those from Mildenhall and

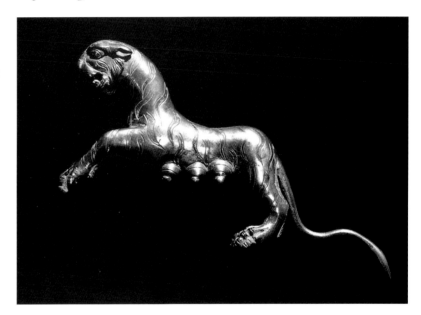

83 The silver tigress, with stripes inlaid with niello, from the Hoxne Treasure, buried in or after AD 407. She is one of two handles from a large silver vase. Length 15.9 cm (6.2 in).

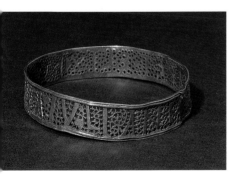

84 A gold bracelet from the Hoxne Treasure. The pierced work incorporates an inscription reading utere felix domina Iuliana, *use [this] happily Lady Juliana. There are 18 other gold bracelets in the hoard. Diameter 6.5 cm (2.5 in).*

Hoxne – was far from uncommon. Similarly, in many of the towns elegant residences, presumably belonging to the decurions (councillors), are a conspicuous feature of the time, especially at places such as Silchester. Now in many instances surrounded by stone walls, urban life persisted, and for some in a relatively luxurious way.

This, however, is not the whole story. Excavation is beginning to show that many of the public monuments in the larger towns entered a period of decay or change from early in the fourth century or, indeed, before. The basilica at London, for instance, was completely demolished c. AD 300, and that at Silchester given over to industrial purposes. Many fora, as at Wroxeter, may also have gone out of use, while it is nowhere possible to demonstrate that amphitheatres were still being maintained as such in the fourth century. Although many of the smaller towns seem to have remained affluent (and were by now often conspicuous centres of industrial production), the main centres had taken on a somewhat different aspect: one reason, undoubtedly, is that the aristocracy no longer felt the need to dig into its pocket to pay for the maintenance of public monuments and festivals.

Much of the security that encouraged the wealthy to build grander town houses and to extend and refurbish their country villas must have resulted from a continued army presence, albeit on a diminished scale. Although Britain was far from free of troubles in the fourth century, successive authorities took care to maintain and, on occasion, even augment the disposition of troops. The best-known aspect of the late third and fourth century defences lies not, however, in the north of England but along the south and east coasts. Eventually to be known as the *Litus Saxonicum*, with its own commander, the 'Count of the Saxon Shore', a number of the fortresses are still finely preserved. One has only to visit Pevensey (Sussex) or Portchester (Hampshire) to appreciate the novelty

85 *Aerial photograph of the Saxon-Shore fort at Pevensey, Sussex. Its massive defences were provided with large internal towers, eleven of which survive, and it commanded a marshy estuary. Recent excavation has shown that it was almost certainly built by Allectus, between AD 293 and 296. In one corner is a medieval castle.*

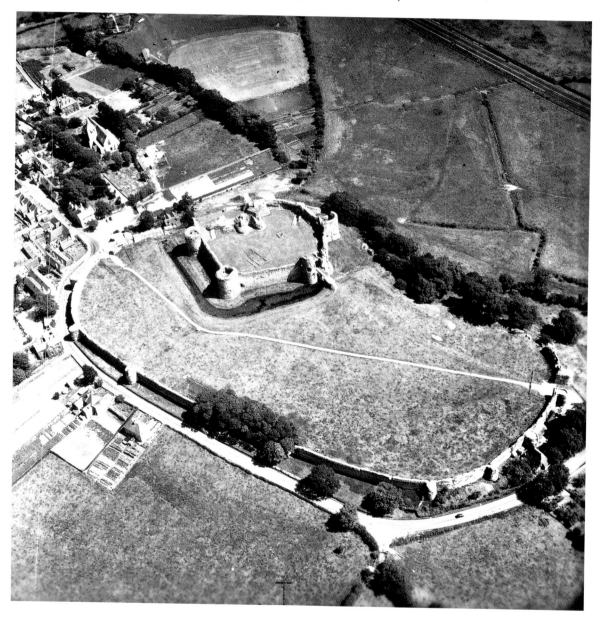

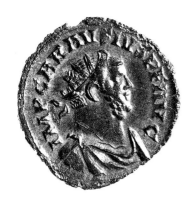

86 *Coin portrait of the usurper Carausius (AD 287-93). He used coinage as a form of propaganda to try to bolster his position, but he was eventually assassinated.*

87 *A partially gilded silver pepper-pot (piperatorium) from the Hoxne Treasure. There are four such vessels in the hoard: this one is designed as a bust of a late-Roman Empress. The type was not uncommon in the late-Antique world as a form for bronze steel-yard-weights, but it is unique as an item of precious tableware. Height 10.3 cm (4 in).*

of the style of architecture: massive high walls, towers both at the corners and along the walls, and strongly built gates. Like the immense defences that characterise so many late-Roman towns in Britain and elsewhere, they represent a fundamental change in policy, from one of attack to one of retreat within fortified citadels.

These 'Saxon-Shore' forts run around the coast from the north-east corner of the Wash as far as Portsmouth and were clearly devised to deal with sea-borne attacks. Others of similar style, such as Lancaster, are also known in the north-west. It has been long thought that many were constructed as part of an overall plan devised by a naval commander, Carausius. He was appointed to stamp out piracy in the Channel and the North Sea but, in AD 286, seized power for himself in Britain. He had been accused of holding on to some of the booty that he had recovered from the pirates, and his usurping of a province may have seemed the only way to defend himself against Roman retaliation. In the event he was murdered in an internal coup, organised by his finance minister, Allectus, and in 296 a Roman army, led by the emperor of the West, Constantius, successfully invaded Britain, and reclaimed the province.

Allectus certainly initiated building work near St Paul's in London – a massive structure with wooden piles dated by dendrochronology pre-

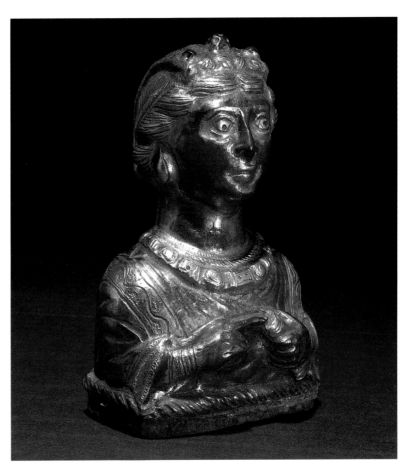

cisely to AD 294 – and recent work concludes that at least eight of the south-eastern forts can be attributed to Carausius (perhaps being finished by Allectus). Although they incorporated some older forts, such as Brancaster, it is nevertheless now clear that they represent a co-ordinated military response to a perceived threat of seaborne invasion, which did indeed eventually materialise: interestingly, this is a verdict at complete variance with that of the first edition of this book, a further affirmation of the transient nature of our knowledge. However, with the crisis of 296 over, and order restored, their subsequent garrisoning may have been irregular and perhaps sporadic; for excavation of sites like Portchester has yielded none of the regularly laid-out barracks, granaries and administrative buildings that typify the forts of northern England. There seems instead to have been a hotchpotch of wooden structures which betray little or no trace of military planning.

To what extent these fortresses played a role in maintaining the prosperity of early-mid fourth-century Britain is, therefore, largely a matter of guesswork. Our historical sources are such that we have only a fairly vague idea of just how frequent and how grave were the disturbances that find occasional mention by ancient writers. We do know of visits by emperors or by very high-ranking military officers in AD 306, 343, 360, 367, 389 and 398, and some were definitely associated with outbreaks of trouble. But the evidence is all too rarely very specific. This is certainly true of what appears to have been the most concerted onslaught by Britain's enemies, the 'Barbarian Conspiracy' of AD 367–8. Here, Picts, Scots, Attacotti and Saxons formed an alliance to launch a simultaneous attack from several different directions. So successful was this plan that the Count of the Saxon Shore was killed and the army of the Duke of Britain all but routed. It took another army, brought in from abroad under the competent command of Count Theodosius, and long campaigning, to re-establish some measure of Roman control.

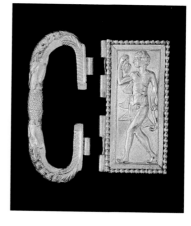

88 Gold belt-buckle from the Thetford Treasure. The figure on the plate is that of a dancing satyr holding a bunch of grapes It is one of a number of explicitly pagan items in the Treasure, which was buried about AD 390, when the empire was officially Christian. Height of plate 5.2 cm (2 in).

89 The twenty-two finger rings from the Thetford Treasure. They typify the flamboyance and love of colour favoured in the late-Antique world. Late fourth century AD.

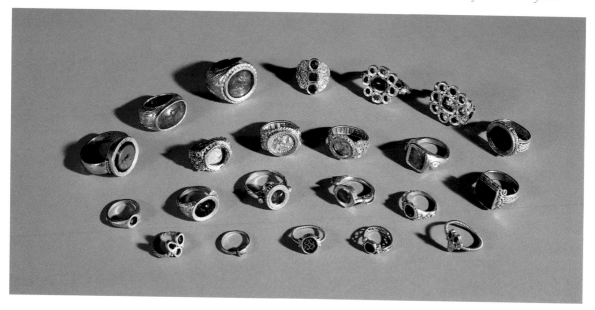

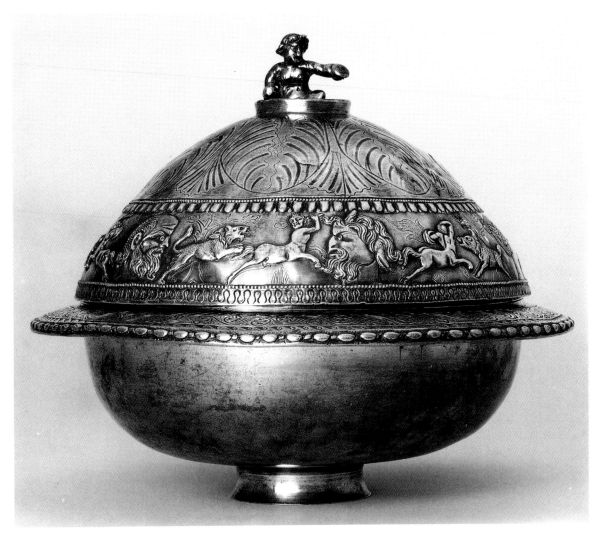

90 *Bowl and lid from the fourth-century Mildenhall Treasure. The lid is surmounted by a triton blowing a conch shell; beneath is a frieze with combats between centaurs and wild beasts, separated by human masks. The bowl is the earliest vessel in the Treasure: the lid has been made for it at a later date. Diameter 22.85 cm (9 in).*

On balance, however, it might be judged that Britain escaped fairly lightly, especially given that there is very little archaeological indication of damage or destruction either in forts or on civilian sites. Until the last decade of the century, when raids by Picts and Scots became so incessant that the great Vandal general, Stilicho, had to mount a prolonged campaign, many Romano-Britons may well have been largely unaffected by the apparent disintegration of the Roman empire around them. It is surely significant that, in the last decades of Roman Britain, this was a country that was producing great thinkers and leaders like St Patrick and the author of the age's most influential Christian heresy, the priest Pelagius; and also collections of metalwork like the Hoxne and Thetford treasures, the latter with its well-informed and intellectual references to a pagan cult described in detail only by Latin writers of some five hundred years earlier. On the other hand, the archaeological evidence is increasingly unambiguous that, in the second half of the fourth century, many of the sites, whether town, villa or sanctuary, entered a period of decline. Once splendid buildings started to fall into disrepair, no longer were mosaicists to hand to lay new floors and, by the 380s, some towns like Isca Dumnoniorum, modern Exeter, had ceased to receive coin. All the indications are that government was falling apart, and that military posts were being increasingly left to their own devices. This explains why great wooden halls were built over the basilica at the town at Wroxeter, and on top of one of the granaries at the Hadrian's Wall fort at Birdoswald. Roman Britain was gradually slipping into a new, early medieval world.

Meanwhile, there were beginning substantial folk migrations beyond Rome's European frontiers. The Vandals, Suebi and others were on the move, and the Saxons and other Germanic tribes were looking upon Britain as an undefended plum, ripe for picking. Rome could give no help and, whatever the detailed story of the first decade of the fifth century, the final severance of Britain from Rome is unambiguous. It is contained in a famous letter of AD 410 from the emperor Honorius to the *civitates* telling them 'to look to their own defence'. He wrote to the towns themselves because there was no army to protect them and no longer any authority to administer them.

Not that this was entirely the end of Roman Britain since there was, after all, still the remnants of a Romanised population. Thus, when St Germanus of Auxerre visited Verulamium (St Albans) in 429, there was apparently an affluent class of city nobles to meet him; here town-life had in some form or other carried on, as indeed has been confirmed by archaeological evidence. But as the Angles and Saxons moved from raiding to settlement, and achieved political dominance over substantial parts of south-eastern England, we can trace a progressive abandonment both of the towns and of many of the rural settlements. Populations surely shrank, and many Romano-Britons will have been absorbed into the culture of the Germanic overlords. Although there was sustained British resistance, irrevocably linked (rightly or wrongly) with the name of Arthur, the breakdown of civic life nevertheless seems overall to have been rapid. Unlike so many towns of Gaul, Italy, Spain and North Africa, there was little compromise between the old and the new order. When St Augustine came to Canterbury in AD 597 to reimplant the Christian faith, he saw not an old Roman town that had somehow survived the Anglo-Saxon invasions but a new one growing up – literally – in the ruins. Roman Britain was to influence Dark Age and medieval Britain in many ways; but it was a very different world that was to emerge out of this obscure province so optimistically created by Rome four centuries earlier.

Further reading

There is a vast bibliography on Roman Britain, which is being constantly extended as new discoveries are made. This brief list includes some of the major works currently available, together with a few more general works, through which it will be possible to find references to more specialist literature. Readers who wish to keep abreast with developments may wish to consult the magazine *Current Archaeology* (available from 9 Nassington Road, London NW3 2TX). There is also an academic journal of Romano-British studies, *Britannia*, which appears annually (published by the Society for the Promotion of Roman Studies, 31-4 Gordon Square, London WC1H 0PP). Also very useful are the short works in the Shire Archaeology series, more than a dozen of which are relevant to Roman Britain; and the series, mainly on major sites, published by English Heritage with Batsford.

Some ancient sources (all available in Penguin Classics)

CAESAR
The Conquest of Gaul

SUETONIUS
The Twelve Caesars

TACITUS
On Britain and Germany

Maps and Guides

ORDNANCE SURVEY
Map of Roman Britain *5th edition, 1991*

ORDNANCE SURVEY
Map of Hadrian's Wall *2nd edition, 1972*

ORDNANCE SURVEY
Map of the Antonine Wall *2nd edition, 1975*

R. J. A. WILSON
A Guide to the Roman remains of Britain *3rd edition, Constable, 1988*

General

L. ALLASON-JONES
Women in Roman Britain *British Museum Press, 1989*

A. R. BIRLEY
The people of Roman Britain *Batsford, 1979*

D. J. BREEZE
The northern frontiers of Rome *Batsford, 1982*

R. G. COLLINGWOOD AND I. A. RICHMOND
The archaeology of Roman Britain *Methuen, 1969*

P. CONNOLLY
Tiberius Claudius Maximus the cavalryman *Oxford University Press, 1988*

P. CONNOLLY
Tiberius Claudius Maximus the legionary *Oxford University Press, 1988*

A. S. ESMONDE-CLEARY
The ending of Roman Britain *Batsford, 1989*

S. S. FRERE
Britannia; a history of Roman Britain *3rd edition, Routledge and Kegan Paul, 1987*

S. S. FRERE AND J. K. ST. JOSEPH
Roman Britain from the air *Cambridge University Press, 1983*

M. HENIG
Religion in Roman Britain *Batsford, 1984*

M. HENIG
The art of Roman Britain *Batsford, 1995*

G. D. B. JONES AND D. J. MATTINGLY
An atlas of Roman Britain *Blackwell Reference, 1990*

J. LIVERSIDGE
Britain in the Roman empire *Routledge and Kegan Paul, 1968*

M. MILLETT
The Romanization of Britain *Cambridge University Press, 1990*

M. MILLETT
Roman Britain *Batsford English Heritage series, 1995*

J. PERCIVAL
The Roman Villa; an historical introduction *Batsford, 1976*

T. W. POTTER AND C. JOHNS
Roman Britain *British Museum Press, 1992*

A. L. F. RIVET
Town and country in Roman Britain *2nd edition, Hutchinson University Press, 1964*

P. SALWAY
The Oxford illustrated history of Roman Britain *Oxford University Press, 1993*

M. TODD
Roman Britain *Fontana, 1981*

Some more specialised books

G. DE LA BÉDOYÈRE
The finds of Roman Britain *Batsford, 1989*

A. K. BOWMAN
Life and letters on the Roman frontier *British Museum Press, 1994*

D. J. BREEZE AND B. DOBSON
Hadrian's Wall *3rd edition, Harmondsworth, 1987*

B. C. BURNHAM AND J. S. WACHER
The 'small towns' of Roman Britain *Batsford, 1990*

W. S. HANSON
Agricola and the conquest of the north *Batsford, 1987*

C. M. JOHNS
The jewellery of Roman Britain *UCL, 1996*

S. JOHNSON
Hadrian's Wall *Batsford English Heritage series, 1989*

I. D. MARGARY
Roman roads in Britain *3rd edition, John Baker, 1973*

D. PERRING
Roman London *Seaby, 1991*

R. REECE
Roman coinage in Britain *Seaby, 1987*

A. L. F. RIVET
The Roman villa in Britain *Routledge and Kegan Paul, 1969*

A. L. F. RIVET AND C. SMITH
The place-names of Roman Britain *Batsford, 1979*

D. STRONG AND D. BROWN (eds)
Roman crafts *Duckworth, 1976*

C. THOMAS
Christianity in Roman Britain *Batsford, 1981*

M. TODD (ed.)
Studies in the Romano-British villa *Leicester University Press, 1978*

M. TODD (ed.)
Research on Roman Britain 1960-89 *Society for the Promotion of Roman Studies: Britannia Monograph 11, 1989*

J. M. C. TOYNBEE
Art in Britain under the Romans Oxford, *Clarendon Press, 1964*

J. S. WACHER
The towns of Roman Britain *2nd edition, Batsford, 1995*

G. WEBSTER
The Roman imperial army *3rd edition, Black, 1985*

Index